the

holy

ordinary

T0273489

the
holy
ordinary

A WAY TO GOD

MARK LONGHURST

Monkfish Book Publishing Company
Rhinebeck, New York

The Holy Ordinary: A Way to God © 2024 by Mark Longhurst

All rights reserved. No part of this book may be used or reproduced in any manner without the consent of the publisher except in critical articles or reviews. Contact the publisher for information.

Paperback ISBN 978-1-958972-51-9

eBook ISBN 978-1-958972-52-6

Library of Congress Cataloging-in-Publication Data

Names: Longhurst, Mark, author.
Title: The Holy ordinary : a way to God / Mark Longhurst.
Description: Rhinebeck, New York : Monkfish Book Publishing Company, [2024]
    | Includes bibliographical references.
Identifiers: LCCN 2024010760 (print) | LCCN 2024010761 (ebook) | ISBN
    9781958972519 (paperback) | ISBN 9781958972526 (ebook)
Subjects: LCSH: Mysticism. | Contemplation. | Spiritual life.
Classification: LCC BL625 .L66 2024 (print) | LCC BL625 (ebook) | DDC
    304/.22--dc23/eng/20240529
LC record available at https://lccn.loc.gov/2024010760
LC ebook record available at https://lccn.loc.gov/2024010761

Book and cover design by Colin Rolfe.

Monkfish Book Publishing Company
22 East Market Street, Suite 304
Rhinebeck, New York 12572
(845) 876-4861
monkfishpublishing.com

contents

preface

For about fifteen years now, I've been on a dedicated path of contemplation and spiritual transformation. Studying theology with some of the world's best thinkers, and earning a degree for church ministry, didn't teach me how to pray. During a season of suffering, I stumbled into my first yoga class, burned out, disembodied, and deeply anxious. Not long after, someone handed me a book by the Franciscan writer Richard Rohr and I became introduced to a path in my own Christian religion that I never knew existed.

I served churches in rural Massachusetts and New York. My guiding aim was to lead declining congregations into experiences of spiritual renewal. I juggled innovative programming and community outreach while trying my best to be present amid committee meetings that ran long and the constant requirement to come up with something meaningful to say every Sunday. It quickly became clear to me then that I would not survive with heart and soul intact as a leader in the church if I did not *walk* the path of transformation myself. Maybe that's an obvious point, but it's one that has changed my life and hopefully made a difference in the people's lives with whom I've worked. I apprenticed my heart to the Christian mystics and haven't looked back since.

Christianity decidedly does not need more heroic spirituality and special, exalted people. We may admire the mystics, but we need a way to make their teachings practical for the rest of us. I consider myself an ordinary mystic because my life looks like many people's lives. I cheer my sons on at their soccer games, go to the movies with friends, work hard at a job I am privileged to love, and watch a little Netflix before I go to sleep. But underneath the rhythmic contours of each day are deepening roots that sip from mystical streams.

I sit in silent meditation, or chant morning psalms, and am reminded at some level that my true life is not found in the things I'm doing. Instead, my belonging lies in the deeper love in which I participate. In such moments, there are portals to divine grace and the ordinary becomes holy. What's more is that I know that there are countless others like me out there. I'm lucky to have met many such people, those who live regular lives on the surface, who are perfectly ordinary in their foibles, but find their soul's purpose in an ultimate reality and love that knows no bounds.

The global crises of our time demand that our spiritualities no longer navel gaze. That's the criticism, at least, of contemplation. How can we pray when the world is burning from fossil fuels and being torn apart by war? To me, it's more urgent to ask, *How can we not pray in times like these?* The true mystics are not those who retreat from the world but who find union with it. We are the ones whose intimacy with God *and Life itself* is such that our eyes are wide open to reality and our hearts necessarily break with those who suffer. We are not ones who flee from reality—but see it, face and transform it. To paraphrase a famous story by Jesus, a mystic cannot cross to the other side when the homeless, the undocumented immigrant, or the refugee, is lying in the road. Union with God means union with each other, the most marginalized, and the planet. Otherwise we're not in union at all.

This book is the fruit of years of study, teaching, and struggling to find a way to honor my soul's desire for depth and relationship with God amidst all the daily demands. These short reflections, usually engaging the Bible, are ways that I have made sense of a deep yearning for God and deep love that I have for life.

I don't want to have a relationship with God (or Reality, or Love, fill in your word) that dwells on the surface. Life is too short and precious. And yet, perhaps like you, I'm not called to live in a monastery and dedicate my days only to solitude and prayer. What I've discovered is that we don't have to become professionally religious in order to *live* as monks and nuns in our hearts. I can be a devoted dad and partner while being fully devoted to Love. I can awaken to Divine Presence in the holy ordinary, and so can you.

part 1

contemplation

SAY YES

Mysticism is the center of Christian faith and the reason why I've stayed a Christian. I'm a preacher's kid and missionary kid who, along the way, questioned everything I received—theology, culture, gender roles, how to read the Bible, you name it. I jumped ship from my childhood evangelical faith for more progressive churches when it became clear that I couldn't support my gay friends as remaining happily so and be welcomed within the evangelical fold.

Eventually, I became ordained and served progressive churches as a pastor. I made many friends and colleagues along my progressive church way, but I always longed for more. To lead a congregation of people seeking God, I needed deeper spiritual formation, more soulful experiences of worship, a broader sense of ancestors in faith, and a way to pray that did not view Jesus only as a political renegade (he is that, but much more) or, on the other spectrum, a magical genie with "five steps for living my best life." That's when I discovered the Christian mystics.

I'm convinced that the mystics of Christianity, and those of other faiths too, struck upon the hidden treasure, the pearl of great price, the core that animates the whole thing. At the same time, mysticism is a foggy concept. What is it, anyway? Too often, just to mention *mysticism* conjures stereotypes. We might think of hippies doing transcendental meditation and claiming "We're all one." Memories passed down from the 1960s linger, such as Beat poet Allen Ginsberg and friends trying to levitate the Pentagon through collective meditation and chant. Or we might write off mysticism as something only isolated desert ascetics, mountain hermits, monks and nuns do. We think that it's irrelevant to daily life for everyone else. Mysticism is something for those *special* people, but it's certainly not for me.

Part of this is due to the way gatekeepers in the Christian tradition have treated the mystics. Instead of celebrating their presence as forerunners of faith, mystics have sometimes been demonized as suspect, as dangerous esoterics that veered from the mainstream norm in favor of cosmic flights of reflection. They've sometimes been deemed heretical, like the brilliant Dominican Meister Eckhart who, after a widely impactful academic career in Europe's most storied intellectual centers, found himself facing charges of "unorthodox teachings." (Let ominous drumroll commence!)

Some good mystics have even been burned at the stake, like the fourteenth century French woman, Marguerite Porete, who refused to recant her reflections on the love of God. Just how can a women's passionate thoughts about the love of God be *that* dangerous? But to religious authorities whose careers depend on a system of external ritual and observance, to insist on the inner experience of divine love is to subvert the system entirely. If I can know God directly, then I don't really need the religious gatekeepers. And the religious gatekeepers don't give up their power without a fight.

I come from the Protestant tradition—to be precise, those serious and often uptight Congregationalists who trace their roots to the New England Puritans—and my tradition does not have an inclusive track record of appreciating mystics. Many of the church's famous mystics lived after Jesus and before the sixteenth century reformers Martin Luther and John Calvin, which meant that no one ever told me about them. My history lessons while an adolescent began with Jesus, continued to the Protestant Reformation, and left all those pesky mystics and Catholics out of sight and out of mind. But Luther himself was formed as an Augustinian monk, well-versed in the church fathers and medieval mystics. He *knew* their teaching, but that didn't stop him from ignoring centuries of wisdom in his passionate but one-sided embrace of Scripture alone. He railed against monks and nuns and called for all monasteries and convents to close. As society and Protestant religion developed, we Protestants didn't feel the need any more to defend ourselves against Catholicism. We simply ignored, buried, and lost our connection to Christianity's mystical heart.

But we're living in an ecumenical era in which those former divisions are no longer ultimate. More of us are realizing that the treasures of Christianity do not belong to one group but are there for all of us to share. Reports crop up of evangelicals praying the Psalms like monks or liberal Protestants walking labyrinths and discovering Eastern Orthodox icons. The practice of Christian meditation has spread out from monasteries across denominations and faiths. Chants from a monastery in France called Taizé have touched hearts all over the globe. The Cistercian monk Thomas Merton became a bestselling author, and we can even buy Trappist jelly at my local grocery store.

So what is it? What is mysticism? On the one hand, it's impossible to define, because to speak about such things inevitably leads to mystery. Etymologically, the Old French *mystique* means "mysterious, full of mystery," and the Greek *mystikos* means "secret, mystic, connected with the mysteries." Mysticism is mysterious, and so when trying to explain what it is, we can find ourselves babbling a bit, like those first Christians in the book of Acts who are overcome by the Holy Spirit and accused of being drunk. *They* knew what they were trying to express, but many of the people around them did not understand. To quote a quip from Augustine of Hippo, when trying to describe time: "I know well enough what it is, provided that nobody asks me; but if I am asked what it is and try to explain, I am baffled."[1]

Here's how one medieval mystical scholar named Jean Gerson tried to explain the inexplicability of mysticism. It is "the experiential knowledge that comes from God through the embrace of unitive love."[2] Somehow a mystic is one whose life experience of an all-embracing divine love causes them to view reality as one. They know from experience that everything is connected. Similarly, the pragmatist philosopher William James stressed mysticism as the "more" of human experience. He wrote a book trying to categorize mystical states from people's direct reports of their experiences, concluding that mysticism is the "mother sea and fountain head of all religions."[3] For Black theologian Howard Thurman, mysticism is "the response of the individual to a personal encounter with God in his/her own spirit."[4] To be a mystic is know God intimately in the deepest places of our heart, soul, mind, and body.

Jesus was a mystic. In John's gospel, which developed a reputation as "the mystical gospel," Jesus' mystical status becomes clear. It is there in the other gospels, too, but John brings it to the fore. Bible readers will perhaps know that Jesus' first miracle (called "signs" in the gospel) is to change water into wine at a wedding in a town called Cana (John 2:1–11). Jesus' mother breaks the unfortunate news that the wine has run out at the party, and Jesus gives a less than charitable reply: "Woman, what concern is that to you and to me? My hour has not yet come" (2:4). Maybe Jesus is just being sexist and rude, but he also might be trying to keep his miracle-worker identity under wraps a bit longer. John's gospel links the "hour" of God's coming to the "hour" of Jesus' death. For Jesus to mention his "hour" at the beginning of the story is to set a foreboding tone. It tells us right from the start that his ministry will clash with the religious and political powers that be.

Jesus is aware that running out of wine at a seven-day Jewish wedding feast is a serious social faux pas. The groom and his family would have been the talk of Cana for years to come. There are Jewish purification water jars nearby, and Jesus tells the servants to fill them with water. Judaism had laws about purity, cleanliness, and when to wash your hands, and these jars would have been set aside for ritual hand-washing purposes. The attendants fill the jars, and Jesus signals for them to take some to the chief steward, who is the wedding's MC. All it takes is one sip and the secret is out: the water has been changed into delicious wine, and Jesus made it happen.

What does all this mean? Jesus' sign is offering us a symbol. It's demonstrating that the systems of religious purity, orthodoxy, and belief (the jars of water) must create space for God's love and mercy to flow (the wine). In the Bible, wine is used as a spiritual metaphor for God's realm, for what English translators of John's gospel called "eternal life" (John 3:16). The writer Brian McLaren renders it more literally "life of the ages," which I prefer.[5] Life of the ages means the era of peace and liberation for which Jesus and his people have been waiting. It means a wedding-worthy celebration breaking into our lives. Jesus trades in the water of religious purity laws and dutiful obligation for the joyful, law-breaking wine of God's embrace.

To borrow a phrase from Franciscan teacher Richard Rohr, Jesus shows that religion is the container to access God, but Spirit and divine love are the contents of the container.[6] The jars of water may be beautiful, but they need the wine to enliven the party. The same is true about the relationship between religion and mysticism. Many people go to church, sing hymns, celebrate sacraments, read scriptures, listen to the preacher, and say the prayers. From a mystical perspective, none of it means very much unless we encounter divine love in our own hearts and lives. Personal experience of God is what all of this is about. If that's not happening, then the party needs more wine.

Love is calling us and the mystic's path is to respond.

.   .   .

BE ACTIVE AND CONTEMPLATIVE

I suspect that the "busy trap" has snagged, caught, or swallowed many readers opening this book. It has certainly snagged me. A career ago, I sometimes wore my busyness as a way of boasting to the world that I am significant and that I matter. I know I'm not the only one. Writer Tim Kreider coined the phrase "the busy trap," and increasingly being busy is not only a trap but a pit out of which one can't seem to claw. But whereas busy people like me once wore their busy business as a badge of pride, Kreider writes that these days instead, "Everyone is still busy—worse than busy, exhausted, too wiped at the end of the day to do more than stress-eat, binge-watch, and doomscroll—but no one's calling it anything other than what it is anymore: an endless, frantic hamster wheel for survival."[7]

I worked ten years as a church pastor, and a wave of anxiety still knots in my stomach when I think of it. I scheduled my calendar to squeeze in as many meetings, pastoral visits, biblical study, and community activities as possible, all with the optimistic hope of not working after the kids went to bed. When, say, sickness decided to rain on my busy parade, my first response was rarely compassion and rest for my weary body. It was, *How long do I have to put up with being bedridden until I can be productive and busy again?*

Why did I take myself so seriously, as if my work required burnout? God, for one, surely does not mind us taking a break. After all, God rested on the seventh day after birthing creation. But my hard-driving, task-oriented psyche did mind and I did not loosen the reigns. The addiction to work and busyness that is widespread in our culture, whether by necessity or compulsion, fills our depths where there would otherwise be joy. Something's got to give.

The gospel writer Luke has a story involving two women named Martha and Mary. Martha is an archetypal character for our time, snagged by the busy trap (Luke 10:38–42). She thinks she is serving God by her many hospitable tasks welcoming esteemed guest Rabbi Jesus. Luke claims instead that her self-perceptions are misguided: "Martha, Martha, you are worried and distracted by many things" (10:41).

Instead of helping Martha, say, place olives on plates and pour wine to welcome Jesus, Mary simply sits and listens to Jesus. Martha is not happy and at first protests her sister Mary's apparent laziness, expecting Jesus to take her side. Martha's been very busy, after all: "Lord, do you not care that my sister has left me to do all the work by myself? Tell her then to help me" (10:40). But Luke has already given the reader a clue to where his priorities lie. In the sentence before, Luke writes that Martha was distracted by her many tasks (10:41). She was pulled in all directions at once, absorbed and busy. Instead of speaking up for Martha's selfless service, Luke's Jesus chides her instead.

Later Christian interpreters used Luke's passage to suggest that the active life is less important and spiritually inferior to the contemplative life. They thought God preferred the still, prayerful, or monastic life over the busy, worldly, and family-friendly life. Early Christian thinkers often read Luke's story in terms of a hierarchy of spirituality, and Martha usually received the short end of the stick. Church fathers agreed with Luke's Jesus and said that Mary took the better path, the higher path. As monasticism developed, sometimes thinkers built entire theologies around this passage to justify their flights towards solitude.

The medieval mystic Bernard of Clairvaux stressed the incompatibility of Mary and Martha, the opposition of the contemplative and active life. He wrote, "Those who give their leisure to God should never under any circumstances aspire to the noisy life of their brethren who have duties to perform."[8] The writer of the fourteenth century mystical text *The Cloud of Unknowing* spoke even more bluntly: "In the church there are two kinds of life, active and contemplative. The active life is lower, and the contemplative is higher."[9] I certainly have many duties to perform and, compared to Bernard's monastery, my house is undoubtedly noisy, which according to the spiritual hierarchy means that I am living a "lower" life. With the weight of Christian tradition solidly behind Mary, what is a busy, modern Christian seeking a holy, ordinary life to do?

Christian biblical interpretation neglected the good and holy worth of work, service, and family. Luke's Jesus declares that Mary has chosen the better path (10:42), but I don't think Luke—or Jesus, for that matter—could quite as easily get away with that today. "How nice for Mary," we might say, "but someone still needs to put food on the table!" Maybe Luke's Jesus is acting like a stereotypical male, ignorant about the effort and logistics that go into running a household and keeping bodies fed. Maybe Luke and Jesus could benefit and learn from taking a day with the kids.

Eventually came the Protestant Reformation and John Calvin overturned the traditional reading of Luke's passage. Calvin wrote a commentary on the gospels and limited the scope of Luke's story. He observed that the passage wasn't about choosing a life calling of either action or prayer; it was simply about knowing the difference between when to listen and when to work. Then, as he often did, Calvin veered to the other extreme. Letting rhetorical excess overflow, he leveled a critique against the monastic life. He said that this passage was wickedly distorted by some to be in favor of the contemplative life, and that "Christ was far from intending that His disciples should devote themselves to idle and frigid speculations."[10] Calvin sneers at the life of contemplation and throws his full support behind action and hard work.

But really, Calvin's is but the predictable critique all busy and work-addicted people level against contemplation. "Stop your navel gazing, you meditators and spiritual seekers! Get off your cushion and do something!" Who has time for contemplation in a world full of crises, needs, and responsibilities?

Rather than condemn or embrace Martha completely, perhaps we should simply show her some compassion. After all, I'm Martha and so are many of you. American culture and much of the global economy is built around Martha's dilemma—and for most of us, it's not even a dilemma. We are stuck neck deep in the busy trap. We seek significance and ultimate meaning not from prayer and stillness, but from our resumés and LinkedIn connections, our networking and brand-building.

Jesus' chiding of Martha in our context becomes a pastoral intervention for obsessive Western over-achievers: "Martha,

Martha, you are worried and distracted about many things" (Luke 10:41–42). Jesus is, in fact, talking directly to me: "Mark, Mark, take a seat and be still."

We are worried and distracted about so very many things. We have so tipped the scales in favor of action that many of us have no idea how to be still, how to rest, how to play, how to be alone, how to be in nature, how to pray, how to make art, how to live a life of meaning and purpose.

Luke praises Mary's choice and ability to focus on one thing. Jesus says, "There is need of only one thing, and Mary has chosen the better part" (10:42). For those ensnared by the busy trap, Mary's single-minded focus can serve as a restorative example. Instead of being pulled in many directions like Martha, Mary is pulled in only one. It is in this way that Martha and Mary, taken together rather than as an either-or choice, represent the evolution from fragmentation to wholeness, from worry and anxiety to stillness and healing.

In contemplative teacher Cynthia Bourgeault's book, *The Meaning of Mary Magdalene*, she shares an Aramaic title that followers gave to Jesus: *Ihidaya*. It comes from an early, Eastern version of Christianity in Syria and refers to Jesus as the whole, single, or Unified One.[11] Christian tradition later used the word to mean a monk or solitary person, the contemplative separated from the world, but the prior meaning underneath was to be unified and whole, single-minded in devotion to God. According to this Aramaic and Syriac tradition, Jesus' early followers were called *ihidayes*, the single ones.

Poking through Luke's story, then, and on the desert fringes of Christianity, we find a profound teaching that does not require us to jettison Martha to sit at Jesus' feet with Mary. It's not a zero-sum choice whether to join the contemplative crowd or to live an active life. For most of us, that's not even realistic.

Even monks have jam to make, beer to brew, accounting to track, and prayer services to conduct. All of us are active, simply by virtue of getting out of bed in the morning. Whether one is still or busy, then, the main fruit of Jesus' message is that of becoming *an integrated person*—whole and single-minded in the focus of one's heart. Jesus says in the non-canonical Gospel of Thomas, "When you are able to make two become one, the inside like the outside, and the outside like the inside, the higher like the lower—then you shall enter in" [to the kingdom of heaven] (Saying 22). In this more esoteric angle on Luke's classic story, the true disciple holds polarities together, and weaves prayer and awareness of God through all actions and hours.

A healthy spirituality holds both Mary and Martha in esteem, honors their unified paradox in each person, and awakens the single-minded heart to God. Such a heart reconciles opposites and makes the two become one. Activists become people who pray without ceasing and contemplatives become people who serve all the time. As Parker Palmer suggests, the choice becomes no longer contemplation *or* action, but rather "action-and-contemplation."[12]

*   *   *

FLEE TO THE HEART OF THE WORLD
LIKE THOMAS MERTON

The Catholic monastic writer Thomas Merton can help those of us seeking to live lives of everyday mysticism in troubled times. Merton was a cloistered monk who wrote passionately from his Trappist enclosure and became a counter-culture hero and spiritual teacher to millions. From his remote hermitage, Merton inspires me to discover God not in fleeing "the world," as if that were possible, but in the daily business of my own ordinary life.

Merton first published a spiritual autobiography in 1948 entitled *The Seven Storey Mountain*. The book became an unlikely bestseller and, although it was not Merton's intent, single-handedly served as a recruitment ad for monasteries across the United States. Merton tells in the book of his conversion to Catholicism and the monastic life. It's a story about a sincere spiritual seeker who turns his back on the contradictions and alienation of modern life in order to find wholeness in the disciplined and sacred severity of the monastery. On a retreat at the Abbey of Gethsemani, in rural Kentucky, Merton glimpsed the grounded cohesion for which he desperately longed—and so he made a radical shift in his life and joined.

His early writings are full of ebullience for the gifts the monastic life can bring. A sense of purposeful awe and unity pervaded his first visit to Gethsemani and he enthusiastically declared the monastery the spiritual "center of America." He surmised, "I had been wondering what was holding this country together, what was keeping the universe from cracking in pieces and falling apart.... It is places like this monastery."[13]

Merton the monk became Merton the writer. He wrote poetry in *The New Yorker* magazine, essays in *Harper's*, and eventually took on topics as wide-ranging as Zen, American Shakers, racial justice, and nuclear war. In the tumultuous 1960s, Merton's voice beamed with laser-like spiritual precision into the many social crises facing America. Only this unique monk, perhaps, could have spoken in chaotic times with such lasting truth and power while, of course, upsetting many. The left chastised him because he did not become more involved in social movements, while the right rejected him for daring to write about political concerns at all. Merton's critical essays on issues such as the Vietnam War, the nuclear escalation with Russia, the civil rights movement, and the ethics of nonviolence pierce through his particular time and place to strike upon the universal. Even outdated, his writings remain prescient. Pick up his book *Faith and Violence* and read his appreciation of Malcolm X and you will think of George Floyd, or read *Seeds of Destruction* to witness a man analyzing racism as a white, privileged Christian problem.

Merton may have lived a cloistered life, but he corresponded by letter with some of the most significant activists, artists, and thinkers of the twentieth century. He traded epistles with folk singer Joan Baez, revolutionary priest Daniel Berrigan, Catholic Worker co-founder Dorothy Day, philosopher Aldous Huxley, Nicaraguan priest Ernesto Cardenal, the Buddhist monk Thich Nhat Hanh, and many more. Merton's essays and letters reveal a man who is profoundly engaged with the pressing issues and questions of his day.

On the surface, his life seems to perpetuate the stereotype that the spiritual life is separate from the active life and that so-called "contemplative" Mary is at odds with so-called "active" Martha (see Luke 10:38–42). Merton's choice to spurn the world to find God in solitude and silence can be perceived as rejecting the lower active life in favor of a higher spiritual calling. And part of this is Merton's doing. Clearly swept away by youthful romanticism, he called the monastery the "Court of the Queen of Heaven."[14] A more mature Merton later admitted that when he entered the monastery, he sought to escape the world's evils in pursuit of heaven's treasure. Merton shows himself on a journey, like all of us, and never fixed in one place.

His monastic conversion story, *The Seven Storey Mountain*, sold copies into the millions and brought the monk fame and

notoriety. Yet he downplayed the book's importance as he deep-
ened in his spiritual journey. He wondered in his book *The Sign
of Jonas* if the "world I am sore at on paper [in *The Seven Storey
Mountain]* is perhaps a figment of my imagination."[15] Then,
years after that, Merton had these self-deprecating words to say:
"Due to a book I wrote 30 years ago, I have myself become
a sort of stereotype of the world-denying contemplative—the
man who spurned New York, spat on Chicago, and tromped on
Louisville, heading for the woods with Thoreau in one pocket,
John of the Cross in another, and holding the Bible open at the
Apocalypse."[16]

He lit upon the paradoxical resolution of the age-old tension between contemplation and action—that the world is not
"out there" separate from us. The world cannot be fled, only
faced in the depths of ourselves, wherever we are. This is a
strange and even miraculous place for Merton to land as, on
the one hand, he became more and more drawn to the hermit's life. In the mid-1960s, he began living in his own hermitage at Gethsemani, but his wide fame still drew many visitors
who came to see him. By 1968, the year of his death, he had
begun casting an eye to California and New Mexico for possible new hermitage sites. He traveled as far as Alaska to consider relocation, which he said was "the ideal place for solitude
and the hermit life."[17] The mystery to be discovered here is
that Merton's perpetual quest for greater silence and solitude
led not to isolation, but to connection. In the encounter with
God in his own soul, he struck upon the inextricable connectedness of all things.

He memorably stood on a street corner in Louisville,
Kentucky while on a break from the monastery walls, and had
an epiphany of his own radiant, divine ordinariness. Having
looked around at the passerby, he wrote:

> I was suddenly overwhelmed by the realization that
> I loved all those people, that they were mine and I
> theirs, that we could not be alien to each other even
> though we were total strangers. The whole illusion
> of a separate, holy existence is a dream.[18]

Contemplation, for Merton, became an awakening to the divine unity of reality that everyone could see—not the private and secret wisdom of a few.

It is not possible, or even desirable, for most seekers of God to live in remote solitude or join a monastic order. I cherish going on retreat and revel in praying the monastic hours, but my true vocation is not to be a monk. My call is simply to be the most loving version of myself. Besides, I'm too busy driving the kids to basketball practice and reminding them to do their homework. Merton matters to me because he shatters the illusory barrier between the world and heaven, prayer and activity. He says, "I do not need to lock myself into solitude and lose all contact with the rest of the world; rather, this poor world has a right to a place in my solitude."[19] Solitude and the world are not at odds or even, in the end, separate. Merton struck upon this truth from one end of the spectrum, by embracing the world as a solitary monk.

Now it is time for those of us more obviously in the world to embrace the monastic depths—which are the depths of grace that God pours forth toward us in all the stations of life in which we find ourselves.

*   *   *

LIVE VIBRANTLY NOW (NOT ONLY LATER)

I first discovered Jesus as the one who saves me from death by offering me life. With a few prayerful words and the fear-inducing aid of an effective evangelistic tract, I swapped my eternal fate of endless torment for an ongoing vacation of heavenly bliss. An image made popular by an evangelical group taught me this zero-sum, eternal choice: two cliffs are separated by a chasm and a cross fits snugly between the jagged cliff edges. God dwells on one side, humanity on the other, and an inseparable gap lies in between the two. In the middle of the chasm hangs a cross, intended to represent the crucifixion of Jesus, which serves as a bridge for me to walk between the cliffs, a path from eternal death to eternal life.

My dad, then a young and serious Congregational pastor, introduced this image to me. The details are fuzzy: I can't be more than ten or eleven, and I think we're seated at a suburban Michigan restaurant table. Dad's explaining the basics of Christian faith to me. Although I don't feel particularly stranded from God, I am learning the equation of salvation: I can't get to the other side, where God lives, on my own. I have no way forward except a plummet to my death or a faith-filled walk across the wooden bridge of Jesus' body on a cross. The cross— with the accompanying invitation for Jesus to join me in my heart—leads me to the other side, saves me, and rewards me with eternal life.

The eternal life I believed I had entered, though, often serves as no more than a spiritual escape hatch. Why bother facing facts about the climate catastrophe if all it takes to move on from this late, great planet is a tract and a prayer? Why bother caring whether poor people have healthcare today when God is our physician in heaven? Why trouble ourselves with protecting land and water, caring for what's right in front of us, when

our spiritual home is not of this world? Why even bother vot-
ing when we're all flying away to heaven in the not-so-distant
future?

I love the Bible and believe God speaks through it, and part
of the way I love it is through struggling with it. John's gospel
is my favorite gospel, and yet it's a difficult read. In John, Jesus
explains his points and tells his tales through dualities: "Light
has come into the world, but people loved darkness," he says
(3:19). Or, even more enigmatically, "flesh gives birth to flesh
and spirit gives birth to spirit" (3:6). The gospel writer has a two-
fold imagination in which there is the world on one hand and
heaven on the other. There is God above and there is earth and
humanity below. There is light and there is darkness. There's
life and there's judgment and wrath. There are outsiders and
there are insiders.

You can understand why many thoughtful people write
John off. In the denomination I served as a minister, I can't
remember many sermons on the gospel of John. Most of the
sermons I heard took inspiration from the so-called "synoptic
gospels," that is, the other three that share similar traits in common, portray Jesus as more of a community organizing rabble
rouser, and are *not* written by John. I get it. It's easier to avoid
what we do not understand or what has been misused. John can
be easily fit into a paradigm that devalues this world, these bodies, and the future of the planet. But the more I've spent time
with John's gospel, the more I'm convinced that we ignore this
gospel to our own spiritual shallowness and detriment. There's
a radiant message here if we can dig below some accrued and
unfortunate meanings.

It all hinges around Jesus' favored phrase, "eternal life."
Countless souls turn to Jesus when enthusiastic preachers or
evangelists quote John's simple and seemingly stark verse, "For
God so loved the world that he gave his one and only Son, that

whoever believes in him shall not perish but have eternal life"
(3:16). Salvation, these preachers teach, is a one and done deci-
sive act. Once you're in, you're in. Say a prayer and *Wham!*
Bang! eternal life is granted and you are handed a golden ticket
to stroll God's heavenly streets. I made multiple trips to those
opportune altars in my own evangelical upbringing, and I
felt lucky and liberated every time. After the ecstatic moment
passed, however, the same doubts and anxieties lingered.

The phrase "eternal life" may conjure images of endless
loops of angelic praise, far removed from the reality in which
we live. I'm pretty sure that at one point in my spiritual journey
I would have welcomed song after song of evangelical praise
music as my version of heaven—but thank God that Jesus has
something more complicated and interesting to say.

You see, in John's gospel, "eternal life" really means *experiencing the life of heaven now, in this world, and then also in the future.*
It is not an evacuation plan for the next world, as author Brian
McLaren says. Maybe we should stop talking about eternal life
and instead use the phrase I mentioned a few pages ago that is
closer to the original Greek: "life of the ages."[20] Or maybe we
can simplify and say that God is always showing up in the holy
ordinary.

In ancient Judaism, people looked forward to a new age
of justice and peace. Many saw the current age, dominated by
Rome, as an age of evil and oppression. God's enactment of the
new age meant an overthrow or "judgment" of the old. There
will be a time, the Hebrew poet-prophets of this new age saw, in
which the wolf will lie down with the lamb" (Isaiah 11:6). There
will be a time when we will beat swords into ploughshares and
weapons of war into farming tools (Isaiah 2:4). There will be a
time when the plundering of the poor will cease and everyone
will have enough. There will be a time when Rome's violence
is overcome by the life-giving power of resurrection—which

in the ancient Jewish imagination was not only about a person being raised, but about a new age being inaugurated. Two ages: one, evil and unjust, dominated by empire and full of suffering; another, glorious and abundant, ruled by God and full of healing.

John's gospel sees the future age of heaven overlapping with the current age. This is why I think of it as a radiant reality shining in the holy ordinary, because eternal life is the depth dimension of life in which we realize that all of it is and has been saturated with the fullness of God. The so-called eschaton (or end of the world, from which theologians get the clunky word eschatology) is upon us, and we do not need to be afraid. We just need to show up to the life in front of us. The life of the end times is being realized now, and it's not the end of the world, it's the passionate beginning! Jesus puts it this way in John: "Whoever believes in the Son has eternal life" (John 3:36). He doesn't say in future tense that the person who believes *will have* eternal life. He says the person *has* eternal life in the present. Whoever awakens to it lives in this new age, the new era of justice and peace and wholeness.

After Jesus meets John the Baptist, John the gospel writer waxes philosophical. It's one of his many head-scratching statements, this time through John the Baptist: "The one who comes from above is above all; the one who is from the earth belongs to the earth and speaks as one from the earth" (John 3:31). On the surface, this simply sounds like more anti-body, anti-world, escapist thinking, but it's not. John's gospel sees reality spatially—heaven is above and earth is below, but that doesn't mean that the two do not overlap. The ages of heaven and earth are connected. It just takes someone being born again, or "from above," to perceive heaven's life in our midst. Heaven and earth are intertwined and yet not all of us are aware of it. It takes an intermediary between the realms to reveal this to us. It takes

Jesus Christ, the Word made flesh, to help us understand spirit and matter's intrinsic union. And once we see, we can't unsee.

This life of the ages broaches the political realm, too. When John calls Jesus the one from heaven, the one from above, he is speaking politically. He's making an authority claim. In theology-speak, sometimes people call this "sovereignty." John says, "The one who comes from above is above all" (3:31). I have cringeworthy memories of fellow Christians claiming Jesus is superior, "above" all other gods, and denying the truth that people on different paths know and bring. But John the Baptist isn't talking about other religions. He's talking about the Roman Empire. John is saying that the Emperor Caesar Augustus, exalted high above all other earthly rulers and enactor of the Roman golden age of imperial peace and prosperity (which is always peace and wealth for some, and war and poverty for others) is not the ultimate ruler. No, the one who comes from heaven above is above all—regardless of monuments and military might. Jesus launches the new age of heaven overlapping with earth, and we are invited to participate in it.

Admittedly, it's difficult to swallow, let alone experience this "life of the ages." There seems always to be more climate denial, more inequality between rich and poor, another mass shooting, more amassing of weapons, and more hatred of those who are different from "us." Regardless of who holds political office, or what we are facing in our lives, John tells us that God's just and peaceful life starts here and now. How we show up to it is up to us.

Eternal life turns out to be far more than a formulaic prayer and an escape plan from reality. Eternal life turns out to be a refusal to allow injustice and even suffering and death itself to have the last word. Another reality, the life of heaven, is upon us. Those who dare to be born again, from above, are those who will live from the boundless joy, the resolute hope, the vigilant peace, and the revolutionary love of heaven's life now.

•   •   •

RECOGNIZE GOD IN ALL PLACES

The line between the sacred and so-called secular cut through music. At least that's how I experienced it in high school. As a pastor's kid, dedicated church attendee and youth group participant, I traveled to the occasional large-scale Christian youth gathering, such as DC '94. At this event, thousands of youth converged in Washington D.C. to scream adoringly during music sets by Christian contemporary musicians like Michael W. Smith or The Newsboys, and attend workshops on the triumphs and trials of being a Christian teenager.

The workshop on "The Devil and Popular Music" is the one that convicted me to my core. The presenter's main point was that popular music is a secret stronghold of the devil. And unfortunately, according to this man, the devil is active in all the *best* music! There was Christian music, on the one hand— represented by the bands singing about Jesus at the conference, and there was secular music, on the other, represented by all the tapes in my tape deck. If I truly loved Jesus, the presenter told, then Smashing Pumpkins, Nine Inch Nails, Nirvana, Rage Against the Machine, heck, even the Beatles, had to go.

This workshop inspired an enthusiastic, nighttime ritual of smashing my tapes and CDs. Several of us from our Lansing, Michigan youth group huddled in a hotel room, my music collection spread out on the floor. We said a few earnest prayers under the dim lamplight, and I demonstrated my commitment to Jesus with all the determined stomping, throwing, scratching, and tape-unspooling I could muster. "Jesus, I give myself to you!" I cried as I crushed Nine Inch Nails's *The Downward Spiral* into pieces—the album I had purchased in the train station on my way to that very conference.

For a while, my passionate rejection of secular music worked. We youth group attendees shared a bond—we were not like those other people, those non-Christians. We were saved, which placed us in a special, knowing in-group. I felt a keen sense of belonging with these teens, that is, until they moved on in their own way, I moved across the ocean to France, and my heartfelt appreciation of diverse music as art remained steadfast in spite of my stated beliefs.

One of the hazards of religion, into which my teenage self and evangelical Christian youth ministry in general plunged headlong, is the tendency to relate to God through divided categories. These categories are always split, and you are either on one side or the other: sacred and secular, church and world, body and soul, matter and spirit, pure and impure. Some people blame it on ancient Greek philosopher Plato and his firm line between the spirit and the flesh; others blame it on Geneva reformer John Calvin and his morbid insistence that humanity is "totally depraved."

Regardless of where it comes from, many who seek God today stumble over a misguided religious vision of *separation:* the belief that encountering God is not natural for us, and that only certain people or certain groups can hope to taste divine presence, provided they travel to certain places, ascribe to certain beliefs, and operate under certain conditions. Designated beliefs and practices spring up that are divided or "set apart"—which are often called *holy*. The severe implication being that we must escape from the ordinary, or at the very least destroy a tape deck, to taste the holy.

In the Judaism of Jesus' day, the entire religious system oriented itself towards the Jerusalem Temple. The Temple was the religious center or axis of the spiritual imagination, the place where God dwelled, where heaven met earth, and where humans had a chance to meet God. Holiness in the temple was spatial and required requisite boundaries. A Gentile (non-Jewish person) could visit the Temple but had to remain in something called the "outer court." A Jewish woman who was not menstruating could proceed into the Temple to a dedicated space. Jewish men could go further. The priests offered sacrifices in a separate area called the "court of priests" and on one day a year, the high priest entered something called the holy of holies, the set apart, central place where God lived. First-century Judaism was not any more obsessed with purity than other religions of the time. Rather, religion itself functioned according to various degrees of separation or division from God.

A separate God requires separated people. The more separate you become, the nearer to the separate God's presence you can be. In the childhood church of a friend of mine, the words "Be Ye Separate" were etched into a prominent stained-glass window. The logic of so much religion, most harmfully manifested in fundamentalism, is that to be close to God is to be separate from the world.

The biblical patriarch Jacob helps us seal these divisions and reclaim holiness in the ordinary. He's an unlikely teacher, to be sure: a grifter and get-ahead fugitive who stumbles upon a direct realization of God. Jacob's name means to supplant or "take by the heel." He grabs brother Esau's heel on the way out of the womb, trying to get a leg up even before he is born

(Genesis 25:26). The firstborn Jewish son in those days is the one who receives the father's blessing and inheritance—we're meant to infer that Jacob angles to steal the birthright before he takes his first breath. And throughout his life, Jacob continues to supplant, swindle, and lie to gain the upper hand.

In the ancient Near East, the father's final blessing conveyed great power and import. With just a few deathbed words, God's favor and the household finances transferred to the eldest son. Once aging father Isaac lay ailing and blind, Jacob seizes his chance—with mother Rebekah's help, no less. He pulls a fast con over Isaac, disguising himself as Esau and compelling his father to offer his blessing for the firstborn's future (Genesis 27). Suffice it to say, Esau does not take it well.

Jacob falls far short of any standards of moral worthiness and yet he has a vision of God while a fugitive fleeing Esau. Jacob doesn't do anything special, go anywhere out of the ordinary, or even really expect to receive his glimpse of holiness. He has a haphazard awakening that provides a humbling message to hearers of his story because it means that imperfect people like you and me can access God whoever and wherever we are. Long before Solomon built the Jerusalem Temple and priests painstakingly created holiness rules, Jacob bumped into the gateway of God, the place where heaven and earth meet. Angels of God visit him, and the presence of God promises him a bright future—all in an anonymous, mundane, and insignificant place.

Extolling divine glory in a temple, cathedral, or pristine mountain view is easy, but Jacob does not discover God's presence at any such places. All that Genesis 28 tells is that Jacob "came to a certain place." At the sun's setting, he lies down in the dirt, pulls up a rock for a pillow, falls asleep, and has a vision of angels ascending and descending a ladder to heaven.

But this ladder is no mere modern stepladder: it's a Babylonian imperial temple, a pyramid or ramp structure that climbs from earth to heaven. The ancient Babylonians called these *ziggurats*, dwelling places of the gods, and only priests were able to enter in. YHWH's boundary-breaking and grace-filled presence does not mind Babylonian religion's divisions and instead launches Jacob's swindling self to the temple's holy gate.

The next morning, Jacob wakes up and exclaims: "Surely the Lord is in this place—and I did not know it" (Genesis 28:6). God's presence is everywhere—can you recognize it? The world is a temple and everyone can access the holy places.

Jacob builds what preacher-writer Barbara Brown Taylor calls an "altar in the world." The divine vision is in his bones and Jacob must respond. He takes the stone that served as his pillow, pours oil on top of it, and fashions an altar to God right then and there. This otherwise unknown altar in an unknown place becomes known and named as Bethel, El Shaddai, the very name for God. Taylor writes:

> Human beings may separate things into as many piles as we wish—separating spirit from flesh, sacred from secular, church from world. But we should not be surprised when God does not recognize the distinctions we make between the two. Earth is so thick with divine possibility that it is a wonder we can walk anywhere without cracking our shins on altars.[21]

Jacob's pillar recognizes and praises the sacred nature of all reality and the holy ordinary. The original purpose of religion—etymologically influenced by the Latin *ligare*, which means to bind or connect[22]—is not to divide, but to unite. Jacob's vision, then, shows religion at its best: threading heaven and earth together. Those who seek a similar awakening likewise proclaim that "God is here in this place, and I did not know it."

Jacob also models authentic prayer. Prayer is not requesting God to be present where God is absent; it is instead the posture and practice of showing up to life by recognizing God's already-present presence. Jacob is the forebear of anyone who reconnects to God and Reality. When we crack our shins on altars and reunite with the Holy One, we inhabit the original intention of religion and rediscover the holy ordinary.

. • •

SHOW UP TO REALITY

Contemplation has charged out of cloistered gates. It once was that faithful renunciates in monastic orders passed down spiritual wisdom, but you had to be in the know to know. Carmelites, Franciscans, Dominicans, Trappists, and more small bands of dedicated God-seekers nurtured Christian mystical lineages and spiritual practices of transformation and passed it on the best they could. They rose at 2 a.m. to sing the Psalms, meditated and prayed with Scripture, kept sustained silence, guarded solitude, cared for the earth, and embraced simplicity, all to keep an inner flame of love for God—who they sometimes called their spouse—blazing. Mysticism has been Christianity's "pearl of great price": usually ignored, sometimes mocked, occasionally suppressed, but for those who swam in Love's depths, fearlessly protected with care.

Today, though, millions of people outside monastery walls practice longtime monastic disciplines. Take, for example, a form of Christian meditation called Centering Prayer. Trappist monks from Spencer, Massachusetts such as Thomas Keating and William Meninger witnessed the American surge of interest in Buddhist meditation in the 1970s. They went back to sources such as the Desert Fathers and Mothers, and the fourteenth century anonymous text *The Cloud of Unknowing*, updated the language, and honed a method Christians could call their own. Centering Prayer is now taught to thousands of people each year.

Call me optimistic, but it seems that if there is to be a global spiritual renewal, contemplation will and must be at the center. Many people in the Global North are bored and burned with church these days, and often rightfully so. Christianity has caused so many wounds that what bears the name Christ has often little to no resemblance to the person. Yet Christianity cannot stop the Spirit's movement and so, despite our manifold failures, the spiritual spark in people indefatigably lives on.

More and more people are honoring the "more" of life by taking up meditation, picking up mystically themed books, attending spiritual retreats, learning yogic breathing, or spending time alone in nature. Teachers who communicate the contemplative path in an accessible way such as Franciscan Richard Rohr, renegade thinker and former Dominican Matthew Fox, interspiritual writer Mirabai Starr, and others have introduced me and us to the vital spiritual fire of ancient mystical wisdom. New generations of people are discovering the depth of religion, even as they toss out the dross.

Something more is stirring, though, than simply mining mystical spirituality and translating it for a wider audience. Thousands of people may sit in Centering Prayer every day, but

a subtle and revolutionary change is also under way. Now that
contemplation has leapt the monastery gates, it takes its right-
ful place as an inner, transforming possibility for all humanity
instead of the keepsake of a few bold guardians. Like reality,
contemplation evolves.

The great heroes and heroines of contemplation teach
us how to enter the narrow gate of intimacy with God, and
sometimes they chart paths toward that end. The sixth-cen-
tury philosopher who went by the name of Dionysius (not
his real name, so we call him Pseudo-Dionysius) suggested
the influential stages of purification, illumination, and per-
fection.[23] Franciscan philosopher Bonaventure, influenced by
Dionysius, did the same. Such mystics affirmed that before one
could reach the heights of loving union with God, a necessary
preparation and awakening must take place. Those charted
paths seem wise to me and yet in these days a broader and
more inclusive contemplative way is also being forged that
builds on the past but welcomes the future. It's a way that ordinary people can discover without feeling like we are failing or
always playing contemplative catch-up.

Here are several definitions of contemplation that writers in
the last fifty years have suggested:

- "Contemplation is any way one has of penetrating illu-
  sion and touching reality." —Parker Palmer[24]
- "The spiritual quest is a fundamental orientation common to the human experience. The commitment to
  seek the ultimate … is imprinted in the heart of the
  world." —Interspiritual mystic Beverly Lanzetta[25]
- "The word contemplation must press beyond the con-
  straints of religious expectations to reach the potential for spiritual centering in the midst of danger."
  —Contemplative teacher Barbara Holmes, suggesting

that experiences of Black suffering and even crises of injustice can startlingly give birth to contemplation[26]

- "A mature Christian sees Christ in everything and everyone else." —Franciscan author Richard Rohr[27]

What I hear above all in these words I trust is that contemplation is fundamentally about *how one sees and shows up to reality*. It is not about how many hours you dedicate to silence, how many prayers you pray, how many books on the inner life you read, the number of retreats you attend, or whether you can say spiritual buzz words and persuade people you are more enlightened than you really are. Contemplation is the liberation process of falling in love with God (or Life, if you prefer), and conversely falling *out of love* with all that hinders our pursuit. This means that contemplation is a quality of our inner lives that can be practiced anywhere, whether kneeling to receive the Eucharist, cooking dinner, or pressing on mindfully toward a deadline at work. It's simply a matter of, as Brian McLaren's podcast title puts it, "Learning How to See."

I do not need to go anywhere to experience intimacy with God. My task is simply to show up where I am with greater receptivity to the present moment. I am praying, yes, when I wake up at 5:30 a.m., sip coffee, and open my prayer book. But I'm also praying when I hike with my dog in the forest or drop my kids at the bus stop. Divine love is available to me and sustaining me whether I am exhausted and grumpy or energized and happy. God is the most hospitable host, always inviting me in, whether I accept the invitation on a given day or not.

What's more is that contemplation includes the capacity to name injustice. The days of the divide between spiritual people and activists are over, and perhaps they never truly existed. If, as Thomas Merton intuited, the world is not "out there" but in my deepest self,[28] then contemplation is not flight from the world but flight to the heart of the world—which is, at the very same time, the heart of God. After all, where else will I find God than in this self and in this reality?

But what is this divine imprint at the heart of reality like (Lanzetta)? To ask that question is to ask how the shape of my own liberated heart will form. And if the scriptures have any-thing to say about it, then the contemplative heart breaks most for those who are marginalized and suffering. To penetrate illu-sion and touch reality (Palmer) is to awaken to the climate cri-sis that Mother Earth and all her inhabitants face due to our unchecked consumption and reliance on fossil fuels. Such prec-ipices for our species require centering in the midst of danger as a daily rhythm (Holmes). Or, contemplation is to lament our embeddedness in systems of white supremacy, and to recognize that Christ is reflected in *every single person* instead of some people and not others (Rohr).

God is always "right here" along with "over there" and the only time to show up is the present.

∙   ∙   ∙

CONTEMPLATE TOGETHER LIKE HOWARD THURMAN

The most memorable worship service I ever led took place in a contemporary art gallery. Chicago-based artist Nick Cave installed a massive exhibition in MASS MoCA, a factory turned cavernous museum located within a short drive from my house. Cave's exhibition, entitled *Until,* engaged issues of racism and police violence in a way that only contemporary art can—through, in this case, hundreds of metallic, colorful ornaments, including sparkling shooting targets—dangling from the ceiling. Part of MASS MoCA and Cave's intention with the exhibit was to create a space for groups in the community to explore its beauty and grapple with its timely themes. So, the good people of my local church and I enlisted help with multiple local artists, the kind permission of the museum, and decided to hold a Sunday morning service there.

The gospel choir from a nearby college greeted attendees with "This Little Light of Mine" as they roamed the exhibit and found their seats. We shared meditative silence and communal lament for our suffering world. A professional dancer interpreted a James Baldwin quotation through movement: "Love takes off the masks that we fear we cannot live within and know we cannot live without." An experimental choir performed. I preached a sermon on the creation of whiteness. We sang more gospel songs.

I can't say what took place, exactly, nor can I pinpoint the transformations that the service incurred. All I can say is that *something happened.* As we gathered, prayed, lamented, clapped, danced, and sang, something that can only be called Spirit-led transpired. We all knew we were on holy ground. Many were moved to tears. It's as if the museum space, the exhibition, the worship, the music, and the community created a context in which our hearts could be laid bare, if only for an hour. We laid our burdens down.

People who participate in religious worship ostensibly affirm that we are turning our hearts to God, offering reverence for divine reality. Sometimes this is true, such as the communal expectation and embodied prayer of Pentecostal churches, or the simple and unpretentious holiness of a monastic liturgy.

Yet in my experience most churches do not expect anything to happen in worship other than what happened last time. Most churches would be shocked if God turned her heart back to us in response.

The influential theologian and pastor Howard Thurman believed that in authentic worship something happens. In fact, Thurman had such a high view of worship that he thought it could help transcend the most polarizing differences. He co-founded the country's first interracial, interfaith congregation in San Francisco in 1944 while segregation laws still held sway. Called "The Church for the Fellowship of all Peoples," a reflection in the church's Meditation Room affirmed:

> Our assumption is that in the worship of God the human spirit stands stripped of all the meaningful, but artificial, barriers that mark off one human being from another. In the presence of God we are not male or female, Methodist, Baptist, Unitarian, Catholic, or Buddhist; German, Italian, Swedish, or African—but human spirits laid bare without any of the pretensions by which, from day to day, we negotiate life.[29]

A philosopher with a mystical heart, Thurman penned sermons and books on experiential spirituality while providing inspiration for some of the most impactful social justice struggles of the twentieth century. Martin Luther King, Jr. is said to have carried his book *Jesus and the Disinherited* in his pocket during the Montgomery bus boycott. Several decades before liberation theology prioritized the experience of the oppressed, Thurman asked what the religion of Jesus had to say to people who live, like Black people in the United States do, with their backs against the wall.

Thurman also helped connect Gandhi's experiments with nonviolence in India with the crisis of racism in America. Thurman visited Gandhi in 1935 as a part of a friendship delegation, discussing with him nonviolent civil disobedience as *satyagraha* or "soul force." Similar to Jesus' teachings about love, Gandhi taught that nonviolence is a powerful force of good that overcomes evil. Thurman brought back to the U.S. the idea of applying nonviolence to America's systemic racism, and the seeds of his encounter with Gandhi would shape the spirituality and strategy of the civil rights movement.

Even as he served as a mentor to many civil rights leaders, at his heart Thurman was a mystic who stressed the vital necessity of the inward journey. Sometimes the left criticized him for not becoming more active in social justice struggles. When challenged about this, he replied frankly, "I'm not a movement man. It's not my way. I work at giving witness in the external aspect of my life to my experience of the truth. That's my way—the way the grain in my wood moves."[30]

At the Church of the Fellowship of All Peoples, Thurman viewed his worship planning through the lens of transformational spiritual experience. Fellowship Church embraced the arts and, while still grounded in Christian faith, the universal wisdom of all religious traditions. A Sunday morning visit to Fellowship Church might have involved communal meditation, a sermon on the Hebrew prophets by a guest rabbi, liturgical dance, worship incorporating early color motion pictures, or a Christmas service involving live models of Madonna and Child from people of diverse cultures. Thurman may not have been on the movement's front lines risking arrest for integrating interstate buses, but he ingeniously created a context of worship for activists to discover their inner resources. He wrote, "to me it was important that individuals who were in the thick of the struggle for social change would be able to find renewal and fresh courage in the spiritual resources of the church. There must be provided a place, a moment, when a person could declare, 'I choose!'"[31]

Mysticism, and all authentic religion, involves choice. We must choose at every moment to refuse to live life on the surface and to plunge the depths of life. To choose this is to drink the wine of God's joy and enter the heart of God's love. There we find, to our paradoxical relief and delight, that the choosing has been done already. It's not up to us and God chose us first—but we wouldn't have known that unless we chose, too.

Thurman also showed that contemplation is not only personal, something to be pursued individually in one's "prayer closet" to the exclusion of other people. I love prayer closets and often hide in them, but contemplation can also be public and communal: The hushed breathing and pause after a rousing song with people, or an inner silence amidst the rhythm and flow of bodies moving in dance. At the end of a yoga class, the participants rest in contemplative silence in *savasana* or "corpse pose" to allow bodies and breath to settle and release. Then there are moments in church when the congregation truly prays together, whether during the Eucharist, or a person's desperate request for prayer. These are times when we say "I choose!" in felt actuality and in the midst of other people.

Howard Thurman prayed in public and community. He surely prayed in his closet too, but he sought in worship services with congregants to experience divine presence and love through prayer, silence, and deep listening. He based his bold experiment of interracial worship in the 1940s and '50s upon the revolutionary expectation that worshipping God together might change people, making them kinder and more accepting of the other. He puts his experience and hope this way:

The qualitative experience I sought for all who shared in the Fellowship [of all People's] community—a search for the moment when God appeared in the head, heart, and soul of a worshipper. This was the moment above all moments, intimate, personal, private, yet shared, miraculously, with the whole human family in celebration. Often there was the need for quiet, for silence, to deepen the collective, corporate sense of worship, and many times during this period in the Sunday services there came "breaths" of waiting.[32]

I planned and led church worship services for a decade, and I can tell you that, sadly, this is not the norm. To contemplate together requires a leader's expanded capacity to see, listen, and perceive what people are experiencing. The liturgy may be elaborate and creative or sparse and simple. The Holy Spirit doesn't care, but she does require us to pay attention. Group facilitators, worship leaders, and ritual creators can all learn from Thurman's bold experiment. Sometimes all it takes is responding in the moment with the right word from the heart to encourage trust and safety. Sometimes the way that a room is set up stifles multiple voices and quells inspiration, and sometimes seating, sound, and spatial design conspire for authentic community to be born. Sometimes music deadens the spirit, and sometimes when voices meet notes, the sounds of heaven on earth ring.

• • •

part 2

connections

CONNECT TO THE SOURCE OF LOVE

The French hills across from Lake Geneva greet me on my return home during boarding school vacation. My sixteen-year-old self rises at 4 a.m., laces up hiking boots, fills a water bottle, grabs a flashlight, and rushes out the door for a ninety-minute, pitch-black hike to the top of the Jura mountains. The Jura mountains run along the Swiss-French border near the towering, snow-covered Alps. My parent's house is planted in these mountains, tucked in a small French village. The Jura are not the Alps, but they provide a breathtaking view of them. Once I reach the top, rays of sunshine sneak over Mont Blanc, the highest mountain in Western Europe.

At this point in my short life, I'm carrying a loaded pack of difficult emotions. My relationship with my dad has hit a rocky patch, I have extreme social anxiety about fitting in at school, and I'm simmering with self-hatred about being perpetually bullied. I reach the top and sit down on a rock. My legs are sore but my heart is overwhelmed by beauty. It's almost as if I've gone beyond myself and tasted unity with something greater. For that brief moment, sun now streaming across white-capped peaks, I experience the truth of the old hymn: "It is well, it is well with my soul." Life is hard but it will be okay. It's these moments that keep me going, moments in which I am reminded that I'm dwelling in and connected to a reality much larger and more loving than myself.

The mystical heart of John's gospel is the divine indwelling. If Jesus has anything to say about it, dwelling in relationship with God might be the secret to living in the holy ordinary. John has a word for this mutual intermingling. He calls it "abiding." We abide in God and God abides in us. Jesus puts it this way to his followers at their last dinner together, "I am the vine, you are the branches. If you abide in me, and I in you, you will bear much fruit; apart from me you can do nothing" (John 15:5). They are connected and one, growing together through and in love.

There's a long Jewish heritage of calling Israel herself the vine. Gospel writer John knows this. Jesus has said previously that he is the temple, and now he claims to be the vine. With astonishing confidence, and not a little controversy, Jesus plunders the most cherished places and metaphors in Judaism and applies them to himself. For prophets such as Jeremiah, vines symbolized ancient Israel, usually wayward and fruitless, having disobeyed Torah and worshipped false gods of security and status rather than YHWH. Through the prophets, God laments the people's spiritual fate by visions of grapes gone wrong: "Yet I had planted you, a red vine of completely sound stock. How is it that you have turned into seedlings of a vine that is alien to me?" (2:21)

Vineyards also call to heart the lover's sigh from the Song of Songs, which in Christian tradition is the allegorical yearning of the soul for God: we read there that "my vineyard is for myself, [my beloved] make haste!" (Song of Songs 8:11-14) Jesus, through John, stands within the collective, symbolic, love-soaked imagery of the vine. "I am the vine," Jesus says, implying that the vine is not political or cultural Israel, and not a religious institution, either. We, all of us, are the people whose hearts make haste to run to the arms of the beloved.

I hear religious people speak about spiritual but not religious people, usually in the context of the mass exodus that they've made from churches. I've witnessed a fair amount of clergy bemoan this state of affairs and offer righteous-sounding pronouncements about the dangers of "cafeteria-style spirituality." But I'm convinced that spiritual but not religious people offer a gift. When churches cease to be interesting, relevant, or to provide space for human transformation; when the church loses the fire of its passion for God; when it fails to be connected to the vine, the source of love, people outside rightfully take things into their own hands and say, "We can love God/Reality/Life, too!" God is revealed in nature through mountains and sunrises. God is revealed in silence, relationships, embodied movement, resistance to injustice, and service to people in poverty. Seekers of the holy, wherever we find them, invite religious people to discover the transformational treasures of relationship with God at the heart of their traditions.

A mystic is one who is connected to the vine. This going beyond the self and receiving of the divine self can take place on ecstatic mountain heights—but more often it happens through the choices we make while doing the laundry or handling disagreements with a lover, partner or friend. Sometimes we need a dramatic experience of love to believe that such love exists. I know I did. Those purple sun rays crowning Alpine peaks seared me with beauty, but then I inevitably had to make the downward trek.

We can be everyday mystics, but first we must understand our capacity for depth and glory. Mystics are not passive, do-nothing, good-for-nothing navel gazers. And while many receive dazzling visions, achieve staggering successes, or endure horrendous suffering, mystics are not simply spiritual heroes whose pinnacles of relationship with God we can never hope to attain. Mystics happen to be my own heroes, but not in the unapproachable sense. Rather, mystics are meant to remind us of our heart's own capacity. As the poet writer Novalis put it, "If all human beings were lovers, the distinction would disappear between mystic and non-mystic."[33]

All of us are potential mystics, which is different from saying that everyone already is one. That's because the spiritual life involves pruning and sometimes fire. Gardeners cut off dead branches to make way for new shoots to grow, for branches to flourish weighted down by plump grapes. Jesus says, "Whoever does not abide in me is thrown away like a branch and withers; such branches are gathered, thrown into the fire, and burned" (John 15:6). I understand this, too. To seek healing, I had to trim and burn a few branches, and it hurt like hell. My long-ingrained self-hatred had to be healed through therapy, medication, loving friendships, a supportive marriage, and deepening experiences of prayer. When he mentions a fire for dead branches, Jesus is not condemning people to infernal damnation—he's describing a process.

To the extent that we live disconnected from the vine, we are cut off from life's fruitfulness. Our souls require cultivation like gardens. Jesus, along with mystic voices from other religions, tells us that our spiritual vitality rests on awakening to intrinsic connectedness. In a time of climate catastrophe, racial justice reckoning, and persistent poverty, the urgency of this awakening cannot be overstated. Abiding in Christ means that we will create systems that support just and peaceful lives for others and for the common good. Abiding in Christ means that we will

unite as one to steward, not destroy, our Mother Earth. How
many branches need to be burned before our vines bear fruit?

.   .   .

LOVE ANIMALS LIKE ST. FRANCIS

I'm not a pet person. I did not grow up with a dog or cat, I never
nurtured a pet beta fish, nor did I ever have the inclination to
pet, walk, or otherwise befriend my friends' animals. Animals,
for me, were out of sight and out of mind. All of that changed
when I met our Bernedoodle Snickers. I drove from Berkshire
County, Massachusetts to Amish territory in Lancaster County,
Pennsylvania, to purchase from a trusted breeder. As I loaded
crate-bound, two-month-old Snickers into my Hyundai Venue,
pocketing her immunization records, I gulped with terror and
realized, *This puppy's life is now in my hands.* The weight of responsibility mirrored the existential shock and joy that dawned when
I first placed my newborn son in a car seat and drove away from
the hospital.

I stopped at a service station for gas and to stock up on
coffee and road snacks. Upon returning, I found Snickers huddled in her crate, shaking with nervous vulnerability. Right then
and there, my heart melted. I loved her and, her eyes locked on
mine, vowed to care for her. Since then, we've potty trained,
visited vets, and attempted to learn not to bark at people when
they come to the front door. I hike with her first thing several
mornings a week. When I do yoga, I cuddle with her in *sava-
nasa.* The most important change she has brought is not only
the caring bond that we share, but the growing, compassionate

awareness of all living creatures. It only took falling in love with one dog for me to greet my friends' cats, chickens, dogs, and even neighboring cows with respect and kindness. Mindfulness for one being expands to mindfulness for many.

From the very beginning of the Bible, the tales tell that we are created for relationship. In Genesis, the Lord God places the human in an idyllic garden and realizes that "it is not good to be alone" (Genesis 2:18). The human needs a companion, so God decides, "I will make him a helper as his partner." It's a touching tale of God attempting to care for the being they have made—and at first failing.

God tries to meet the needs of the picky earth-person known as Adam. God forms the animals of the field and the birds of the air, and like a child showing a parent her drawing, God brings them to the human to see what they think. I can imagine God presenting an eagle and asking with tenderness, "Do you like it?"

God does the work of creating animals and hands over to Adam the task of naming them. What shall the human call these creatures? Adam may have pondered the meaning of each being or simply stated whatever first came to mind: "Whatever the human called each creature, that was its name" (2:19). Giving names in the biblical world is a way of ordering reality—presumably the human is noticing and naming differences of fur, teeth and claw. But none of the creatures eases the loneliness. The human throws up hands and says, "I still haven't found the one." Apparently, Adam's needs for companionship are quite particular. No animal makes the cut—not even man's so-called best friend.

It's a sweet story that touches our longing for companionship with another human being, and yet even in this earthy and intimate story, the animals still end up having value only insofar as they relate to the human being. Religion has not yet evolved to the place where animals exist as good in themselves. Animals have to exist *for us.*

St. Francis of Assisi, on the other hand, is famous for seeing non-human animals as a part of his family, as his kin. Francis marks a moment in Christian tradition in which animals move from being "other" to animals being "brother" and "sister." He preached to birds, refused to step on worms, and cared especially for sheep, as they reminded him of the Lamb of God. Granted, he also cursed a pig who killed a lamb and called flies "instruments of the devil," but instead of viewing humanity as having dominance over creatures, he saw all life related and as one.[34]

At a church I led in the Berkshire hills of Massachusetts, we held a "Blessing of the Animals" service each year. We prayed for people grieving the loss of pets who have since died, even building an altar with photos of deceased pets. We invited kids to cart their stuffed animals to the front of the sanctuary to be blessed. A woman once brought a huge Newfoundland dog. Another woman brought her horse in a trailer to the front church entrance to receive a blessing. People frequently brought their cats. One boy brought lizards. We blessed these animals in the name of the Creator, the Christ, and the Holy Spirit.

There's a famous legend about St. Francis involving the so-called wolf of Gubbio. Gubbio is a little town in Italy. The story goes like this: a wolf is wreaking terror on the town. Not only does this big, bad wolf eat animals from the town, but it also eats people. From little pigs to town elites, everyone is terrified by this monstrous wolf. People no longer roam freely in the countryside, but they carry weapons and, even then, their weapons do not protect them.

Francis goes out in search of the wolf, even though the townspeople advise against it. When the wolf sees Francis, he predictably charges towards him with a voracious, teeth-baring mouth. Francis's response is not to flee or fight, but instead to make the sign of the cross and talk. Francis says, "Come to me, Brother Wolf. In the name of Christ, I order you not to hurt me or anyone. Brother Wolf, you have done great harm in this region. You deserve to be put to death, and the whole town is against you. But, Brother Wolf, I want to make peace between you and them, so that they will not be harmed by you anymore."[35]

According to the legend, it works. Francis and the wolf stroll together into the center of town, in front of a waiting crowd, to demonstrate the peace they have made. The wolf and Francis join hands, affirm the wolf's newly found nonviolent commitment, and the town's fear is turned into inclusive reconciliation; they commit to feeding and caring for the wolf as long as it lives.

This is a saintly morality tale, a legend developed over centuries. Some think the wolf represents a bandit harming the town. Others see a more inner invitation: perhaps fellow Franciscan friars told this tale to encourage each other to make peace with their struggle against their "animal instincts" of anger, lust, envy, and pride. Yet Francis's friendship with the wolf, a predator the town deemed terrifying, is a reminder of humans' inherent kinship with creation. Eco-theologian Thomas Berry writes that our task "is to reinvent the human—at the species level, with critical reflection, within the community of life systems."[36] Humans are one frighteningly powerful species that happens to exist within a community of other living beings. We are not above, over, or outside of relationships with animals.

It is long past time that we humans find our appropriate, downsized place in the community of life. We have much to learn, as the Hebrew Bible character Job does, from animals—and perhaps we will only recognize the dignity of fellow living creatures when we come face to face with the ecological suffering we have wrought. You may recall that Job is the one who has his health, family, home, and job stripped away from him, with God's permission. And when he asks God, "Why?" the response God gives is simply: "Ask the animals, and they will teach you; the birds of the air and they will tell you." (Job 12:7-10)

.   .   .

LIVE A GREEN LIFE LIKE HILDEGARD OF BINGEN

If I head down a local route and drive for two miles on a spring day, I will encounter acres of earthly heaven. The flower garden is a rainbow of colors, the sprawling fields are harvesting bountiful tomatoes, kale, and carrots, and the Berkshire hills are nobly rising in the background. If it's a farm distribution day, a calm and purposeful bustle pervades the grounds as kids run and play, and old friends stop and chat while sorting kale and plucking raspberries. It's a green place, dreamed and tended by two friends who have lived green lives.

Sam and Elizabeth moved to western Massachusetts in the 1960s to teach in a small high school, but they soon became fully absorbed in a different life calling to farm vegetables. Journalist Ann Larkin Hansen tells their story: what started with a garden, baby chicks, and several other animals soon expanded to become thirty-five acres of visionary greenness called Caretaker Farm. Sam, Elizabeth, and Caretaker Farm became important leaders in the burgeoning local and organic farms movement. As Elizabeth recalls, quoted by Hansen, "We were deeply troubled about the direction our country was moving in, the way our children were being educated, how our food was being grown, and where it was coming from. We realized that our whole food economy was based on oil. A group of us began a local food-buying cooperative, which places monthly orders to this day."[37]

Their effort, along with other like-minded lovers of the land, started what became the Northeast Organic Farmers Association (NOFA). They sold vegetables, opened a bakery, and brought on farming apprentices. Over the years, Caretaker Farm began one of the early CSA (Community-Supported Agriculture) models in the country, in which local community members purchase "shares" of the farm's yield—thereby providing delicious, organic vegetables to local families, as well as a reliable income for the farm.

When I met Sam and Elizabeth, they had retired from farming after thirty-five years, but still lived in a house on the farm. Even their retirement choices demonstrated their resolute commitment to caring for the earth. Handing off farming duties to a new generation of farmers, they worked with a non-profit and the state of Massachusetts to ensure the land would be dedicated to farming legally and permanently. Sam and Elizabeth had always participated in political action, environmental marches, and local efforts of earth-stewardship, but retirement freed them up even more for organizing and education efforts. They supported our church's divestment from fossil fuel investments, demonstrated against pipelines, and led small discussion groups about climate change and faith. Passionate and joy-filled, they could always be counted on for a thoughtful walk or cup of tea, a robust theological discussion, or to fill me in about the latest environmental politics.

Twelfth-century German mystic Hildegard of Bingen lived a green life. A mystic uniquely attuned to ecology, Hildegard was an earth-centered prophetess of greenness. A unique concept she calls "greenness," in Latin *viriditas,* springs forth through her writings. The word finds root in the Latin *virido*, which means "to make green" or "to grow green." Translators don't quite know what to do with Hildegard's greenness, because she uses "*viriditas*" to describe all manner of aliveness. Freshness, vitality, fecundity, fruitfulness, and growth are all green. *Viriditas.* The word is a summation of Hildegard's theology: the whole universe is green, pulsing and sustained by the Spirit's evolving life force.

Hildegard possessed many gifts and accomplished much. She experienced visions (and wrote about them), composed music, ran a convent, practiced natural healing, preached to clergy in a time when women rarely did so, wrote medical texts, invented her own language, and created a play. She was so unique and her output so productive and diverse that scholar William Harmless describes her as a mystical multimedia artist.[38]

Hildegard's greenness does not only traverse the ecology of heaven, but grounds down in earthly dirt. Plants and trees and fields and the natural world are all green, and yet green matter is not separate from spirit. After all, God is the source of greenness, animating Adam and Eve and all of us with greenness, too. In one of her famous hymns named "O greenest branch," Hildegard honors Mary's fruitful greenness in giving birth to Christ—and then through the Incarnation, "there appeared, in greenesses full, all things. Heaven's dew dropped down over the grass and all the earth grew glad."[39] God and the universe green together.

Greenness grows in Hildegard's work similarly to how John's gospel affirms life. Life in John's gospel is both physical and symbolic, earthy and ethereal. A royal official journeys to Jesus in Cana, the same site of Jesus' first water-to-wine sign. The official's son lies at his home in Capernaum—a day's journey away—at the point of death. Jesus assures the man that his son will have life, "Go, your son will live" (John 4:50). The man takes Jesus' word for it, and his attendants meet him on the return journey home to share the vivifying news. Jesus' ministry is a life-giving force that heals bodies, provides sight, and multiplies bread for thousands. Jesus even commands life's re-emergence from Lazarus's tomb of death. The divine life pulsing through Jesus culminates, of course, in God raising him up after life is extinguished.

Like Hildegard, John's gospel eagerly emphasizes that divine life is the sustaining source of all life. Matter is not all there is. Matter exists with spirit because everything that is originates from and lives in God.

John's gospel begins with a life-affirming burst. All things came into being through the Word (1:3), John writes, but then specifies that what came into being is vitality itself: "what has come into being in him was life, and this life was the light of all people" (John 1:4). The coming of Christ, Hildegard might say, is green. Jesus says, "I have come that they may have life, and have it abundantly" (John 10:10).

As I've mentioned throughout, though, many people have heard John's gospel used in a way that vanquishes life and dries out verdant soil. They omit the love that God has for *this* life— "God so loved the world"—and turn "eternal life" (3:16) into a heavenly space ticket out of here. The planet is "late and great," according to 1970s writer Hal Lindsey, which is a convenient way of escaping our shared responsibility to honor and steward life.

Divine life in John may seem otherworldly but it is not later. As Richard Rohr puts it, eternal life is not "chronological moments of endless duration" but "time as momentous and revealing the whole right now."[40] Eternal life in John is a vibrant reality in God in which the ongoing moment of God's life is revealed today. It continues tomorrow, too, but Jesus' good news is that God has thrown open the doors of heaven's realm right now. And if we sap life's greenness now, odds are that we will ignore its fruitfulness later.

Hildegard's visionary book the *Scivias* ends with a heavenly choir singing of Mary as a "sweet, green branch" and Christ as the "glorious Flower."[41] And yet the soundtrack of heaven is not an angelic chorus running on repeat. John and Hildegard share a vision of the divine life's fresh abundance. Such greening starts now, grows in our lives and, watered by grace, continues its blooming into the life to come.

The jagged edge of the spiritual journey, however, is that our lives often are *not green* but dry. John would call many of us spiritually dead or dying. Hildegard puts it ecologically by calling on greenness's opposite—not *viriditas* but *ariditas*, which means drought or dryness. Greenness is the goal but seasoned farmers like Sam and Elizabeth can always tell stories of tragically ruined harvests. "Anything devoid of life-force is dead," Hildegard says, "just as a limb cut off from a tree becomes withered."[42]

Our souls are sometimes barren, disconnected from divinity's growth. Instead of fresh newness, life sometimes becomes one thing after the other. Our passion dies, our creativity becomes blocked, we become stuck in deadening habits and, before we know it, we are less alive, expectant, hopeful, and green. For Hildegard and Jesus, the Holy Spirit is always bursting forth in our world, a fountain of abundant aliveness.

A green life bears fruit, continuing the human vocation to "be fruitful and multiply" (Genesis 1:28). Fruitful people fulfilling a fruitful vocation reveal an ecological greenness of soul. They effuse fruits of Spirit, which the apostle Paul lists in Galatians as love, joy, peace, patience, kindness, generosity, faithfulness, gentleness, and self-control (Galatians 5:22-23).

The corridors of religion often become constrained, but Hildegard's genius is to embed the life of faith within the language and world of nature. Following a green God in a greening world means that God, the world, and humanity are not unchanging, but always sprouting seeds of new possibilities. Hildegard inspires us to a life attuned to the earth and awakened by God, a life that does not simply exist but flourishes bountifully.

. . .

MAKE SENSE OF ANGELS LIKE A SCIENTIST

The universe is weird. Here are a few weird and startling science facts I stumbled across in a book entitled, *What a Wonderful World.* The author winsomely explains facts that I otherwise wouldn't have had a clue about, such as:

- We share a third of our DNA with mushrooms.
- If you squeezed all the empty space out of all the atoms in all the people in the world, the entire human race could fit inside the volume of a sugar cube.
- We age more slowly on the ground floor of a building than on the top floor.
- Dark matter makes up 24% of the energy of the universe—and we have no idea really what it is.
- Every day our bodies create 300 billion new cells, more than the number of stars in the Milky Way.[43]

The progressive Christian circles that I've run in, however, are not very weird. They're reasonable and respectable, like going to the local rotary club. We affirm the parts of our faith and tradition that make sense to us, and we don't feel too bad about ignoring the parts that don't.

Things like spiritual healing, angels, demons, and resurrection from the dead make non-religious people and even many Christians queasy. Many people leave Christian faith because they just can't believe that events like a virgin birth could take place. The literal level of reading is the *lowest* level of meaning, said early church fathers, but we box ourselves in with the choice to either affirm or deny. There are certainly those who run headfirst into religiously weird corners and abandon facts and rationality. The majority of Christians I've spent time with, though, often ignore the weirder parts of religion completely— or shrug them off as outdated aspects of a crusty old faith that we don't need anymore.

What if we reclaimed weird again? What if faith was at least as weird as the universe in which we find ourselves—and the universe, remember, is *really weird?*

One song that reverberates through my evangelical upbringing to this day is from a Christian pop star named Amy Grant, which goes, "Angels watching over me, every step I take." I had written this song and sentiment off for years. Angels watching over me? I don't think so. But now that I've been finally finding a way to reconcile science and religion, Christ and the cosmos, I've started to become curious about angels again. The more I learn about the strangeness of the universe, the more I'm curious to delve into the oddities of my religion. I've even been wondering if angels really *are* watching over me.

Angels in the Bible are messengers who often turn out to be surprising visitors, from Abraham and Sarah's hospitality to three unknown men (18:1-15), to Jacob physically grappling with a mysterious man at the Jabbok River (Genesis 32:22-32). The angel Gabriel, just as weird, has become famous from announcing his big, messianic pregnancy news to Mary (Luke

1:26-38). Angel Gabriel's previous appearance in the Bible is to explain to Daniel a wild, bizarre vision involving rams, goats, and the rise and fall of empires (Daniel 8:15-26).

The letter to the Hebrews reminds readers of angels' surreptitious anonymity: "Do not neglect to show hospitality to strangers, for by doing that some have entertained angels without knowing it" (13:2). What if these messengers are real in some weird way today? What if they still bear God's news of love and justice? What if they somehow tell the truth of who we are? To ask such a question is exploratory by nature. I can't prove it, but what if the strangeness of the universe itself invites such pondering?

Angels on holiday cards and Christmas decorations are made trite by sentimentalism and bad art. Those of us with critical minds will ask for factual truth, but that often proves elusive. How do you prove you've seen an angel? I haven't seen one yet, but if I talked to my therapist about seeing them, I can imagine he might insist kindly that my winged visions have more to do with the seer than the seen. "Let's talk about what these angels mean for *you*," he'd probably say.

After all, not everyone can receive visions like Hildegard of Bingen. Plus, angels in the Bible evoke fear much more than joy when they show up (Luke 2:10). Which makes me ask: do any of us *really* want to encounter an angel? They're not cute. In fact, they disrupt lives, or at least break through the ceiling, like the angel at the end of Tony Kushner's play *Angels in America*.

If you asked an ancient person how the universe works, they wouldn't have the tools to tell you much that would hold scientific weight today. But odds are that they would bring up angels. The Bible simply assumes we live in a universe in which the veil between heaven and earth is thin, and heavenly intermediaries or messengers frequently traverse the boundaries.

The Book of Jubilees is an ancient Jewish book that early Christians read but never put into their Bible. It has a whole

angelology, which is a fancy word for an actual theological field
that studies belief in angels. Yes, you can get a PhD in angels,
which doesn't mean you actually have seen one or would know
what to do if you did. In the Book of Jubilees, angels offer praise
to God in heaven, they are there at the creation of the world,
they narrate the contents of the Torah (Jewish scriptures), and
they even assist God with planning divine missions. They dwell
as personalities over the elements. There are angels of fire,
winds, clouds, darkness, snow, hail, hoar, frost, cold, heat, thun-
der, lightning, and seasons (Jubilees 2:2). Isn't that cool?

Such cosmic presences might seem far-fetched to reasonable minds today, but really, every time we act, speak, or pray as
if nature has *soulfulness* to it, we are affirming angels—or at least
an angelic function. The writer J. Philip Newell reminds modern spiritual seekers of the earth-centered wisdom of the Celtic
tradition. One of his books contains daily prayers that might as
well be called angelic nature prayers: "The strength of the rising sun, the strength of the swelling sea, the high mountains, the
fertile plains, the strength of the everlasting river, the strength
of the river of God, flowing in me and through me this day."[44]

Angels are more, though, than the spiritual dimension of
rocks and rivers, the mysterious figures ascending and descending Jacob's visionary ladder (Genesis 28:12), or lingering know-
ingly inside Jesus' empty tomb (John 20:12).

Angels are also tasked with representing whole peoples and
nations—whether for good or for ill. In Deuteronomy, God
divides up the nations and assigns an angel or "son of God" to
each people group" (Deuteronomy 32:8). The book of Daniel
contains a vision in which an angel visits Daniel—another
weird, anonymous visitor. This visitor tells how he was delayed
in responding to Daniel's prayers because he was busy fighting
another angel, the angel (translated "prince") of Persia (Daniel
10:12).

Theologian Walter Wink describes the ancient cosmology
of angels representing whole peoples as "a kind of systems-view
of international politics under the aspect of God's final sovereignty."[45] We can track the politics of the ancient world, in other
words, by paying attention to angels. In the book of Revelation—
the science fiction-horror genre mash-up that I'm convinced is
the most interesting book of the Bible—the prophetic visionary John of Patmos is exiled on an island and writes letters to
the seven angels of the seven churches. He doesn't write letters
to the pastors of the churches—he writes them to the *angels*.
Angels can serve healing ends for the collective good; they can
also serve unjust, imperial ends and become their counterpoint
"demons"—which are *angels that lost their way*.

What might angels of communities and peoples look like
today? What angels have "fallen," lost their vocation to serve,
and become demonic instead? What joys and wounds do our
angels carry? What might the angel of the United States, where
I live, be telling us—if indeed she still is good? What might the
angel of Earth be trying to communicate? To push the boundaries of this thought exploration even further, what is science to
make of angels? Does the weird world of spirit correspond at
all to the weird world of science, or are we firmly in the realm
of unmoored conjecture?

What kind of world do we inhabit?

In the seventeenth century, about a hundred years before
Charles Darwin, scientists followed Isaac Newton in affirming that the universe functioned like a cosmic clock. It followed ordered and reliable rules, as theologian-scientist Ilia
Delio puts it: "In Newton's world the sovereign, omnipotent
God governed the world from above and the cosmos ran like a
machine according to internal laws and mechanisms."[46] Fields
like astronomy began to grow, and scientists began studying,
categorizing, and learning ever more about the universe. At the

same time, scholars began turning the scientific method to the study of the Bible itself, naming contradictions between the text and the observable world, ferreting out the phenomena they deemed unrealistic and that never could have happened. The impact of this scientific revolution is that much of the mystery and magic of both science and spirituality went underground. Newton himself studied the occult but had to keep it a secret.[47]

But whereas religion once boldly explored the weirder dimensions of our inner and outer lives—whether in medieval mystic Hildegard's green universe or early church philosopher Dionysius the Areopagite's "celestial hierarchies" of angels—today it's as if the sciences have evolved to be far weirder than faith. Religion in mainline Christianity is often rational, ordered and predictable, operating like predictable clockwork, and now it's the universe that is truly hard to believe.

My point is simply this: angels can help us recover the weirdness of faith. After all, what if the weirdness of faith is not separate from the weirdness of the universe? It's not my goal to convince you to believe or disbelieve. I hope instead to invite you to a trusting posture toward God and the universe that embraces inexplicable strangeness. And I'm convinced that this mysterious and weird universe might just reciprocally embrace us back.

.　　.　　.

LOVE LIKE MY GRANDMOTHER (AND THE TRINITY)

My grandmother Margaret Longhurst overflowed with love. She raised and put up with three raucous boys: Jimmy, Bobby, and Ricky. She also loved faithfully and put up with her dependable but controlling and cranky husband George, whom we called Poppy. Margaret and George lived self-reliant lives. They built their house and nurtured sprawling backyard flower and vegetable gardens. If it could be grown, odds are that Grandma grew it. She tended tomatoes, cucumbers, lettuce, and squash, along with bees and raspberry bushes. She baked fresh bread every morning and canned in the fall. Her garden didn't only serve the immediate family, it served the entire Latham, New York community. Neighbors and churchgoers received buckets of tomatoes and quarts of blueberries and Margaret's zinnias decorated the local church entryway. If someone Margaret or George knew found themselves in the hospital during flower season, they could count on a fresh, hand-picked bouquet delivered to their room.

Margaret Longhurst's love didn't flow because she accomplished much. She was whip smart, but not successful in any field. For years, she longed to attend college or become a schoolteacher, but never had the chance. In later decades, she seemed depressed and exhausted. One night at the summer lake house she mentioned with wistful sadness her desire to travel and see more of the world. She followed her unguarded moment with a predictable resignation, "Well, George probably wouldn't agree to it."

To observers, her life was ordinary and simple. And yet, Grandma's actual life was *holy ordinary* because to encounter her was to encounter love and kindness itself. It wasn't only her deeds of service that exemplified her love, although it was that. Her presence pierced you. When she looked at you with her big eyes through her big bifocals, chatting and asking questions about your life, her big heart radiated. Then she invited you in for a cup of tea and a game of Scrabble.

The doctrine of the Trinity, the oneness of God expressed through the three persons of Father, Son, and Holy Spirit, is notorious for its impenetrability and apparent irrelevance to everyday life. But when I think of the Trinity I think of my grandmother, because the Trinity is God's love overflowing. The Trinity's doctrinal history finds its most memorable moments in relational metaphors of ecstatic love, of love that always flows beyond itself. The Trinity is like a waterfall, said Franciscan mystic Bonaventure, in which God's love overflows from the fountain-fullness of Father, as he put it, to the Son, to the Spirit, and to all creation.[48] The Trinity mirrors the best of human love, said Scottish theologian Richard of St. Victor, in which the love between two cannot stay contained, and so it shares love with a third.[49] Flemish mystic Jan van Ruusbroec envisioned the Trinity like a constantly moving whirlpool, in which the Father, Son, Spirit, and universe all participate together in what I suppose you could call the hot tub "jets" of God's love.[50]

John the gospel writer didn't have the pleasure of knowing my grandmother, nor would he have recognized "Trinity" as a fully developed category for describing God. Yet when theologians debated the three-in-one identity of God in the fourth century, they turned not to Matthew, Mark, or Luke, but to John. The three "synoptic" gospel writers presented an earthy Jesus: a teacher, a prophet, a nonviolent revolutionary, and a miracle worker. Instead, John sees Jesus as a "heavenly man" sent from "above" to reveal God's glory and grace; a human-divine being who somehow shared "equality" with God. "I and the Father are one," he said (John 10:30).

Jesus shines through the prism of divine, overflowing love. You can be renewed in Spirit through a second birth, he tells Nicodemus (John 3:3). Later on in John chapter seventeen, Jesus prays: "As you, Father, are in me and I am in you, may they (the disciples) also be in us" (John 17:21). Right there, John plants seeds of the Trinity through the mutual indwelling of the Father and Son. But it's not a narcissistic love that they share, gazing in each other's eyes like star-struck lovers without a care in the world. Instead, this divine love creates room for another, for the Holy Spirit, for Jesus' disciples, for us, for creation, and for the world.

The earliest Christians, like John, mirrored different proto-Trinitarian possibilities, but they were too concerned with imperial persecution, martyrdom, and basic survival to clarify their ideas in any cohesive way. It would take the Emperor Constantine's conversion, the peace brought about by Rome's rule, and the bitter power struggles of Christian bishops to articulate a formal doctrine of the Trinity.

Theologians lost sleep at night thinking about the philosophical relationship between God the Father and God the Son. Was Jesus the Son of the same substance as God the Father? The fourth-century Council of Nicaea, convened by Emperor Constantine himself, took the strong position of yes. But who's going to vote no when the emperor is present? Only two had the courage to do so. Or was Jesus subordinate, less powerful than and created by God the Father? The infamous heretic Arius seemed to think yes, as did his followers in Alexandria, who chanted his popular slogan: "There was when he was not."[51] There was a time when Jesus the Son did not exist, he thought, when God the Father dwelled only in indivisible unity and mystery.

And what's the point of Trinitarian doctrine, anyway? After all, the fourth century disputes devolved into something ugly. Bishops campaigned for their theological perspectives as if it were a Pennsylvania primary. They lobbied the emperor to have opposition bishops exiled. They honed messaging with sound-bite slogans. They played dirty politics: the enemies of one bishop in Antioch, for example, had him deposed by convincing a woman to stand up in front of a formal synod gathering, hold her baby, and declare that the baby was the bishop's son. He was, predictably, labeled a heretic and adulterer and sent into exile. His real sin was taking a harsh stand against the followers of Arius in a politically unpopular moment. On the woman's deathbed, the legend goes, she confessed that the rival bishops had paid her.[52] There are low points in Trinity's evolution, and there are high points, too.

Margaret Longhurst did not train in theology. She did not know a thing about Arius, the other famous bishop Athanasius, or that bishop in Antioch. She didn't reflect on the once-contested, now forgotten nuances of divine Father and Son. She had children to feed, a household to run, and a garden to tend. Yet she demonstrated why the Trinity matters today because she overflowed with love. Through the thickets of argument and politics and Greek philosophy and patriarchal language, that's what the Christian tradition testifies God is like—God is like my grandmother.

When we overflow with love, like a waterfall or whirlpool or ecstatic lovers, we participate in that ancient Trinitarian rhythm. We join with God, three-in-one, in loving the world.

· · ·

SING TO THE COSMIC CHRIST LIKE JOHN MUIR

Overflowing with love like the Trinity leads to praise. I'm convinced that it's not only my grandmother through whom such love flowed, but nature and reality itself. I'm not often given to effusive praise in my prayer, but I can't help it here:

Praise!

Praise God!

Praise reality.

Praise the cosmos.

Praise color. Praise paint.

Praise bodies, animal, human and celestial.

By whatever name you call the endless depths,
Christ and all sacred names, praise.

People who discover the holy ordinary are those who allow wonder and praise to sing through their lives. They are often those we call saints, prophets, artists, and mystics.

John Muir is one such wonder-filled man. Born in Scotland, in 1838, to a stern Christian minister, his father beat him while preaching about moral, behavior. Even from a young age, John Muir felt that his true home and church was in nature. He dropped out of college, suffered a temporarily blinding accident in an Indianapolis factory, and then spent time wandering the country somewhat aimlessly. Shortly after the Civil War, he walked a thousand miles from Indiana to the Gulf of Mexico. He walked from San Francisco to Yosemite.

From his playing in the forest as a boy to trekking mountains as a man, he is filled with passion for nature's beauty and majesty. The only language he can come up with to describe his experience was that of deep spirituality.

He says that Nature baptizes him.[53]

He says that mountains at dawn are cathedrals.[54]

He says that each drop of rain is God's messenger, an angel of love.[55]

He calls Yosemite a temple and the sounds of its waterfalls, psalms.[56] This is the language and heart of wonder. It is also the language of the Cosmic Christ.

The Bible is full of songs to the Cosmic Christ that John

Muir might appreciate. One is known as the "Colossians Canticle": "For in him all things were created, in heaven and on earth, visible and invisible, whether thrones or dominions or principalities or authorities—all things were created through him and for him" (1:16). Monks around the world chant these verses to this day.

The Colossians writer claims that "all things are created through Christ, and for Christ"—or, as the Greek reads, *towards* Christ[57]—which is to say that Christ is there at the beginning of it all and at the end of it all. Christ is the Alpha and Omega, as the book of Revelation puts it (22:13). The Spirit hovers over the deep waters before the first day, and Christ is there amidst the unformed chaos. The universe first expands, coalescing within hydrogen clouds, and Christ is there stirring forth stars. The new heavens and new earth are unveiled, death itself has passed away, and Christ is there at the end. It's a "Christ-soaked universe," to borrow a memorable phrase from Franciscan author Richard Rohr.[58]

But let me back up a bit. Many of us do not know about the Cosmic Christ, have not been taught about the Cosmic Christ, and might even be slightly skeptical about what a "Cosmic" Christ has to do with the human one. Allow me to follow a biblical trail to explain.

Christ is not Jesus' last name, says Rohr in another place.[59] In fact, Jews in Jesus' day didn't use last names like we do today. Following his Jewish custom, Jesus would likely have been identified by his father's name, his birthplace, or even his occupation. If you asked someone where Jesus Christ lived, no one would be able to provide a response. But Jesus son of Joseph, Jesus of Nazareth or Jesus the carpenter? "Sure," the neighbors might say, "he's down there by the Galilee shore."

But if Christ is not Jesus' last name, what does it mean to call Jesus "Christ"?

Christ is a not a name, it's a title. The English rendering "Christ" comes from the Greek word *Christos*, which itself is a translation of a Hebrew word that means Messiah (*mashiach*). Christ is the Messiah, we might say, except to say that is really to repeat ourselves. Saying Christ is the Messiah is akin to saying simply "Christ is the Christ," when what we probably mean is that Jesus is the Messiah.

The earliest Christians affirmed Jesus as the Messiah, the longed-for ruler in Jewish imagination who will bring salvation and institute a realm of justice and peace. This Messiah will save the people by welcoming the exiled and dispersed and by overthrowing the foreign empires that always seemed to be breathing down ancient Israel's neck. Jesus is the Messiah, these first Christians said, the Christ.

To follow the etymological thread further: the Hebrew word for Messiah (*mashiach*) means "anointed." Ancient Jews anointed objects and people with oil as a way of dedicating them to a holy purpose. God tells Moses to anoint all the sacred tabernacle items, from altar to table to lampstand to covenant ark, with oil (Exodus 40:9). The prophet Isaiah cries, "Get up, you officers, oil the shields!" (Isaiah 21:5) Make them slippery for battle, so that God protects the people from flying arrows and enemy swords.

Most memorably, though, priests anointed kings with oil to designate them to the divinely-given role of ruling with justice and compassion. The prophet Samuel anoints David with oil to be king (1 Samuel 16:13) and a priest named Zadok anoints David's son Solomon when it is his time to rule (1 Kings 1:39). At a particularly low and bloody point in Israel's history, the priest Jehoiada anoints seven-year-old boy Joash to be king (2 Kings 11:9–12). All this kingly anointing meant that priests poured oil over the person's head in a symbolic ritual to dedicate their reign to God. I'm one who believes that Christianity's monarchical language and hierarchical associations need to be traded in for new inclusive and egalitarian metaphors—I far prefer to pray to Jesus as "Brother" or "Beloved" than "Lord"— yet to call Jesus the Christ is partly to join this ancient tradition and name him a king. The anointed one.

For the writer of Colossians, though, Jesus the Christ means far more than an Israelite king. Jesus is Christ and Messiah, to be sure, but also "the image of the invisible God, the firstborn of all creation" (1:15). The meaning of Christ stretches from the kingly to the cosmic. Jesus is here the face of the divine mystery and the first creative act birthed from that mystery.

But what does such a cosmic Christ have to do with the human Jesus? What happened to Jesus, the trouble-making son of Joseph? Isn't this Jesus born from Mary and brother to James? Isn't Jesus known for telling subversive stories called parables, the one who insistently heralds the arrival of God's realm? Isn't he the nonviolent revolutionary who performs a direct action in the Jerusalem Temple by interrupting the commodities trading?

Yes, Jesus is Jesus, son of Joseph and Mary, the very same carpenter from Nazareth known for dining with the excluded, compromised, and desperate. At the same time, Christians throughout the centuries have affirmed that Jesus is also the Christ. "All things were created through him and for him" (1:16), lifting Christ up to the level of the heavens.

The letter to the Colossians, written around the same time as the Gospels, presents Christ in a position of paradoxical power. He's the one who is put to death, through whom "peace is made through the blood of his cross" (Colossians 1:20), but who rules over all authorities and empires, galaxies, and multiverses.

In other words, Christ is ultimate. But Christ need not be ultimate in a Game of Thrones, "Bend the knee or die" type of way. Christ is instead, to borrow a phrase from theologian Paul Tillich, our "ultimate concern." For the Colossians writer, to claim that "Christ is before all things and in Christ all things hold together" is to say that all reality is saturated, filled with, *concerned* with, "soaked" with Christ. To follow the Cosmic Christ as one's ultimate concern is to pledge fealty to this vast and benevolent reality, and correspondingly to let go of what, in the end, is *not* as ultimate.

In the circles in which I've participated in ministry, it's easy to become comfortable with the historical Jesus. The historical Jesus is the one that we can prove through critical research traveled here and there and said thus and so. He represented a subversive threat to the establishment by leading a "poor people's campaign" from the margins—and his radical inclusion and generous love galvanizes our hearts still today. Many of us are familiar with and love this Jesus. This Jesus and his way of love and justice propels our lives.

He was a Jewish, popular teacher and healer charged and killed as a Roman seditionist. But some Christians become stuck in history by treating Jesus only as a museum to visit, and not an inspirited-universe in which to inhabit. What if the activist, non-violent revolutionary Jesus is only half the story? What if there is a larger and more whole vision through which to see reality? What if our historical Jesus is too small, and we are missing out on the expansive scope of Christ's breadth and depth (Romans 8:38-9)?

The Colossians writer and readers sing: "Christ is the head of the body—the church, Christ is the beginning, the first-born from among the dead" (Colossians 1:18). Can you catch how the author leads with an effusive, cosmic statement, and then adds the very localized word, "church"? Christ is the head of the body—but the body is far larger than the church. One commentator is convinced that the author inserted the word "church" into a pre-existing hymn to the Cosmic Christ because the hymn's praise sings that the cosmos and Earth are the first body of Christ.[60] The universe is alive with God, expanding and contracting with God's own rhythms, anointed to be of service and filled with divine presence.

The recognition of Christ in the world has to start somewhere, and where better to start than the gathered, local community we know as church? But we turned church into the exclusive body of Christ instead of recognizing its participation in the larger universal body of reality. If Christ has been there from the beginning and all things were created through him and towards him, then we go to church to be reminded in community that the world is filled with God, and that this Christ imprint in all beings is recognizable. There, and wherever we go, we can sing like John Muir.

.   .   .

JOIN THE RESURRECTION MOVEMENT

Notre Dame Cathedral burned the week I wrote this chapter. There she was on our phone's feeds and TV screens: Our Lady and her timber spire and wooden roof, unimaginably ablaze. Hearts broke while friends and I relived memories from visiting that sacred place, some having travelled there with family as a child, and others who backpacked across Europe. Amidst the fire, the cross and altar stood surrounded by ash, proclaiming the Paschal Mystery itself in naked symbol. Through death and disaster, God dies with us. Through death and disaster, God rises with us. Having withstood the French Revolution, World War I, and the Nazi occupation of France, it is only a matter of time before Paris's Lady, like Jesus, will rise again.[61]

The mystery of Christianity is that our dyings and risings

are bound up with one another. Three other churches likewise burned around the same time as Notre Dame. These churches, located in Louisiana, did not burn because of a possible electrical fire, but because of white supremacy. Their fires might otherwise have disappeared in the perpetual march of the media's "now," but the collective grief of Notre Dame's burning helped raise their profile. A denominational association set up a GoFund me fundraiser for the Louisiana churches—before the Notre Dame fire, their fundraising totaled just over $100,000. After the Notre Dame fire, they surpassed the $2 million dollar mark.[62]

Each year Easter is, for Christians, a celebration of the rising of Christ, but this rising is far more than one person's death-defying divine act. The resurrection of Christ is expansive: Jesus the person rises and launches God's resurrection movement that brings everyone and everything along with it.

It starts with a body or, rather, a body's absence. Mary Magdalene and other women are at the tomb before sunrise to preserve Jesus' body with spices (Luke 24:1). A rolled-away stone ensures they can enter the tomb easily, but the body is missing. Two men—angels—stand near them wearing clothes that dazzle like the very lightening of the sky. They point out the befuddled obvious: "He is not here" and the more shocking, "He has risen" (24:5).

Jesus Christ rises first on Easter morning to the women. Shortly after, he will make appearances to two disciples on the road to Emmaus (24:13-35) and to disciples gathered in Jerusalem (24:36-49), but it's the women who first see the empty tomb and believe. Jesus Christ rises to Mary Magdalene, the devoted disciple extraordinaire, to Mary the mother of James, to Joanna, who—Luke chapter eight tells us—is married to the manager of Herod's household himself, and to the other women who were with them at the tomb (24:10). You could

even say that the women are rising with Jesus. They are the first
to witness the empty tomb, the first to herald a new message of
hope, the first to glimpse a renewed world where love is stronger
than death.

At their moment of proclamation, Luke lobs the unfortunate line: "this seemed to them [the men] an idle tale" (24:11).
The women have excitedly passed along the resurrection news
to the male apostles but—as happens predictably in patriarchal
cultures—the men do not believe the women's experiences. We
can hear James, John, Philip, Bartholomew and the rest say
something amounting to, *You women must be imagining things. An
empty tomb does not make sense. If I don't see it, I don't believe it.*

But the implications of the empty tomb are not seen by
those looking for an eyewitness investigative account of what
did or did not happen. Only those whose hearts bear the capacity to love can see the resurrection and dream a new way out of
no way. The men lack this consciousness—Luke says they "did
not believe them" (24:10). It's to Peter's credit that he follows
his awakening heart, still bruised from his threefold betrayal of
Jesus, and runs to check the tomb himself. Perhaps he hopes for
a last-ditch chance to demonstrate his faithfulness. Perhaps out
of aching desperation, Peter is rising, too.

Jesus Christ rises, except that many in the Christian religion
have turned this transformational tale into an individual heroic
feat. He did it, or God did it on his behalf, and we are amazed
at the miracle of it all. Jesus becomes our Marvel Studios box
office juggernaut: after disappearing briefly to another galaxy,
Superman Jesus is back from the dead to save us. Others in
the Christian tradition often take an alternative approach: we
ignore the resurrection completely and awkwardly downplay
its importance for faith. We celebrate it on Easter Sunday but,
like kids eating beets, it's only because someone else told us we
should.

Jesus rising, however, is only the beginning or "first fruits" of resurrection (1 Corinthians 15:20). In Jesus Christ, God's resurrecting movement has begun, and it sweeps everyone and everything up within it. Dying and rising are a central pattern and truth of reality—and so to talk about Jesus' rising is somehow to approach the weighty paradox of death and life evolving together at the center of the universe. Mary, Joanna, and the other women are rising, Peter is rising, I'm rising, you're rising, and the universe itself is rising. Resurrection, as Wendell Berry tells in his classic "The Mad Farmer Liberation Front" poem, is humus building under trees, sequoias planted, choosing love over profit, the sheer bliss of resting in a lover's arms in a field, the practice of believing and enacting that another world is possible.[63]

Scholars Sarah Sexton Crossan and John Dominic Crossan traveled the world researching resurrection painting traditions and discovered a universal vision. In their book *Resurrecting Easter: How the West Lost and the East Kept the Original Easter Vision*, they show how painting traditions in Eastern Orthodoxy picture Jesus rising up from Hades in the underworld and bringing others along with him. Jesus often stands over the cross, a distressed Hades gatekeeper usually glaring on from below, and has hands outstretched so that Adam and Eve rise up too. Kings David and Solomon and John the Baptist are sometimes there, among other biblical characters that make appearances in the paintings.[64]

This artistic tradition tells us that resurrection is not only for one body; it is for all. Resurrection is the collective rising up that includes the amazing feats that will take place to and through all humanity. Jesus Christ leads the way, and we all participate. Justice rises for all bodies, especially bodies that most suffer, such as trans bodies, queer bodies, incarcerated bodies, homeless bodies, and Black bodies.

Those two Crossan researchers tell in travelogue, detective style how they went to Moscow to view an ancient Psalm book. Known as the "Khludov Psalter," and discovered in ninth century Constantinople, artists created illustrations to sit alongside the psalmists' prayers. Crossan and Crossan examined pictures in dusty margins and realized that the resurrection scenes are placed next to prayers for God to rise up against injustice.[65] Images of Christ risen from the tomb appear connected with verses such as: "Rise up, O Lord; lift yourself up against the fury of my enemies," from Psalm 7:6. "Rise up, O Lord. O God, lift up your hand, do not forget the oppressed," from Psalm 10:12. The rising of Jesus Christ is intimately connected with the rising up against oppression, and the pairing of ancient illustration and Psalm teach us this central Easter truth.

Jesus rises, but then brings everyone else with him, including creation itself. The scope of resurrection matters, and it's not limited to Christians, nor is it limited to human beings. The Easter vigil in the Roman Catholic Church prays: "Exult, all creation, around God's throne; Rejoice, O Earth, in shining splendor."[66] This universal resurrection is led by women, joined by the poor and marginalized, and includes all humanity, the earth and cosmos. It is a Christ-movement of new possibilities and new worlds.

*   *   *

liberations

CHOOSE JOY

In Central Square in Cambridge, Massachusetts, Little Joe Cook and his rhythm and blues band The Thrillers boogied on Friday nights. After a long week of reading theology texts, my housemates and I descended on The Cantab Lounge ready to let loose, and Little Joe Cook and friends did not disappoint. In his mid 70s at that time, Joe Cook had been a fixture of Cambridge music for years. The place packed, Joe Cook—known as the Peanut Man from his 1957 pop hit single "Peanuts—joined his band's throbbing bass, popping trumpet, and sly keyboard to host one of the most joyful live music nights I've been a part of.

He sang regular songs like "Down at the Cantab," the words of which many had memorized. "You can have a ball / one and all," he insisted. "All you got to do is get up from your seat / Start movin' your feet." And we did. I am an anxious, heady person by temperament, at that time disconnected from my body, and made more so by reading hours upon hours each day in divinity school. I did not dance easily or gracefully. Usually I stood nervously for the first hour sipping my craft I.P.A's, watching the evening revelers, jealous of their joy. Eventually the crowd's enthusiasm, a friend's cajoling, or the beer buzz dragged me to the dance floor—where I wanted to be. Once moving, I found my feet, my body found its flow, and my joy swelled.

Dance night at The Cantab stirred up joy while my studies at the divinity school often swirled with stress. My classes and book piles gifted their own type of liberation by widely exploring realms of religion, asking questions that I had never before dared to ask like, "Why has Christianity been at the heart of so much violence?" and "Why were some gospels included in the Bible and some left out?" But while freeing, I can't say that I experienced much joy in my studies and preparation for ministry. My anxiety kept me too on edge all the time, and I had not yet discovered tools like yoga to help calm my worry. At The Cantab Lounge, though, I partied with joy. Little Joe Cook knew something that my theology books did not.

In John's gospel, we are introduced to Jesus' joy early on at a party at the wedding celebration in Cana. I'd like to think that the wedding guests danced and sweated like my friends and I grooving with the Peanut Man. Cana is located in a region called Galilee, which in John's gospel is where the joyful things happen. The tragic events like Jesus' betrayal and death will take place towards the end of the tale, a bit further south in Jerusalem. In Galilee and at the beginning of the story, wine flows from water.

Given the unfortunate Christian tendency sometimes to smother joy, it's worth saying that this party is an actual party. Some interpreters on one end of the spectrum have humorously tried to say that Jesus only turned water into grape juice, but let's not kid ourselves. Jesus' first so-called "sign," through which he reveals divine glory, is to turn water into wine. I'm not sure what my teetotalling grandmother—the same one who revealed the love of the Trinity to me—would have made of this one. Jesus, like all his family and friends, is Jewish and follows

Jewish laws and customs, which included joyful letting loose for weddings. In first century Israel, weddings could last for seven days and involve the whole town. Generally, the groom's generous patronage supplied the plentiful wine.

The wine is wine but it is not *only* wine. Wine served not only as a social lubricant for wedding dancing, it also provided a joyful symbol of justice for ancient Israel. The little patch of earth known as Palestine had been pawned off from empire to empire. The Assyrians conquered the northern kingdom or "Israel" in the seventh century BCE; the Babylonians conquered the southern kingdom of "Judah" in the early sixth century. They handed the people Israel to the Greeks, and then they handed them to the Romans.

Gospel writer John mixes all these associations when Jesus attends the wedding in Cana and performs his memorable sign. The wine runs out and Jesus' mother, unnamed at this point in the story, conveys the socially disastrous news. While it may seem trivial to us today, running low on supplies was no laughing matter to the groom. Should his drink have dwindled, he would have been the laughingstock of the town, dishonored in front of his friends and family.

Jesus takes water pots used for Jewish purification rituals and turns the pure water into wine. The Jewish wedding attendees don't seem to mind, but John already has clued readers into who it is who will take offense—the Temple leadership and their network of supporters. We might chuckle at the uptightness awkwardness of religious people unwilling to party, but just imagine if revelers used the church's silver communion chalices to play beer pong. *Then* who would be irate? Jesus tends to court controversy.

There's something about joy that seems inherently destabilizing. Why do religious people have such a reputation for being staid and serious more than we do for being jovial and joyful?

Fundamentalists decry dancing, but it's not as if conservative Christians have the market cornered on joylessness. In my days as a progressive pastor, like the religious leaders in Jesus' day, I often noticed a skepticism of spontaneous joy. Religious folks—and speaking as one myself, for better or worse—are the ones who need our vestments and liturgical colors laid out in just the right way, our communion planned out just so, our Robert's Rules of Order followed to the tee. And for those of us who care deeply about the world's crises, there can also be a subtle guilt around experiencing joy: How dare we, or how can we, be joyful when there is so much to worry about, so much to do, so much going wrong in our world and our lives?

The joy Jesus uncorks, however, is not simply a temporary refill for our empty cups, a diversion from the sense of unfulfillment in our lives. Nor is it a superficial joy cultivated by the insulated bliss of privilege. Jesus' joy is more akin to what folk singer Bruce Cockburn describes as "this fluttering joker dancing in the dragon's jaws." We're meant to hold this joyful banquet up alongside the daring and sometimes deadly confrontation with evil that justice brings.

There is, after all, an ominous reality mixed in with the free-flowing wine: Jesus is aware of where his actions will bring him. "My hour is not yet come," he says in reply to his mother's request to intervene in the groom's wineless debacle (2:4). "Hour" in John's gospel comes loaded with symbolic baggage, associated with the crucifixion as it is. Later in the book, Jesus will face his impending death and pray to God, "Now my soul is troubled, and what shall I say? Father, save me from this hour! No, it was for this very reason that I came to this hour" (John 12:27). Yet Jesus changes the water into wine anyway. Jesus chooses joy, as Wendell Berry puts it, even though he has considered all the facts.[67]

I think of Alyosha, from Dostoyevky's epic novel *The Brothers Karamazov*, standing over his Eastern Orthodox teacher Father Zossima's coffin. During the funeral, he hears the Scripture passage of the Wedding at Cana being read, and oddly enough, Alyosha dozes off to sleep. He finds himself swept up in a surreal vision in which he is at the wedding of Cana, too. He sees the bride and bridegroom, the host of the feast, the village poor, his deceased elder teacher, and there they all are rejoicing and drinking the new wine of gladness. After he wakes up from the vision, he rushes outside, falls on his knees, and begins weeping and kissing the earth. He hears an echo in his soul, which says, "Water the earth with the tears of your joy and love those tears." The new wine of the wedding party is flowing freely to us, and it stirs a joy that is stronger than death.

.   .   .

LOVE LIKE JAMES BALDWIN

I'm convinced that the writer James Baldwin is a prophet for our troubled times. A Black, gay, revered essayist and novelist, Baldwin became a public intellectual known for his searing insights on race, religion, sexuality, and what it means to be an American. He combines a fierce critique of systemic racism in the United States with a relentless and deeply biblical vision of love. But Baldwin's love is not a sentimental love that's avoidant or ignorant of the world's crises. Rather, Baldwin's love is the creative and sometimes terrible force that fuels inner reckoning with truth. Love that leads to change. His character Vivaldo asks in *Another Country*, "How's one going to get through it all? How can you live if you can't love? And how can you live if you do?"[68]

James Baldwin published a short essay entitled "My Dungeon Shook: A Letter to My Nephew," which is included in his acclaimed book *The Fire Next Time*. In 1962, he is reporting from Senegal for *The New Yorker* magazine. He travels throughout Africa and encounters the masses of people, the colors, and the poverty, along with the moral bankruptcy of the elite, political class. But what is really on his mind is the United States. Somehow the geographical distance that he takes from his own country allows him to find the words for his experience of race in America.[69]

"My Dungeon Shook" is first a love letter. Baldwin writes to his nephew "Big James" to tell him that he is loved. "Here you were: to be loved. To be loved, baby, hard, at once, and forever, to strengthen you against the loveless world."[70] Part of the way Baldwin knows how to love his nephew is to tell him the truth of what it means to be Black in America: "This innocent country set you down in a ghetto in which, in fact, it intended that you should perish…. You were born where you were born and faced the future that you faced because you were black and for no other reason."[71] Baldwin's love faces reality, even if that reality turns out to be a racist nightmare. He's convinced that "Love takes off masks we fear we cannot live without and know we cannot live within."[72]

The letter of 1 John is one of three tiny epistles in John's name tucked away towards the end of the Bible. There is much about the letter of 1 John which lends it to the Bible's end obscurity: its shortness, for one; a chapter dedicated to announcing the coming antichrist, for another. And yet this brief book contains some of the most famous verses about love in the Bible: "This is the message you have heard from the beginning, that we should love one another" (1 John 3:11). Martin Luther King Jr. called for an international fellowship of people united across differences of race, class, and nation and quoted 1 John, "Let us love one another, for love is from God" (1 John 4:7).[73] From the beginning of their embattled community, 1 John's readers have heard one consistent message, modeled by the one consistent witness of Jesus: love one another.

The next verse reads as a counter-example to the love Jesus-followers must offer: "We must *not* be like Cain, who murdered his brother" (1 John 3:12). The Genesis text that 1 John references mysteriously never says *why* Cain's sacrifice displeased God, or why brother Abel's sacrifice pleased God (see Genesis 4:1-16). Rabbinic commentators were happy to fill in the gaps, though—Cain brought ordinary fruit to sacrifice, they said, rather than the first fruits of the harvest. He brought the leftovers. Either way, so the story goes, Cain becomes jealous and kills his brother. Abel's blood, Genesis says, "Cries out from the ground" (4:10)—just as the blood of enslaved Black bodies or murdered Indigenous bodies cries out from America's ground.

"Do not be astonished, brothers and sisters"—or, we might add, Baldwin's nephew James—"that the world hates you" (1 John 3:13). The world may enslave you, imprison you, murder you, steal from you, but know, the writer says, "that we have passed from death to life because we love one another" (1 John 3:14). Love liberates us from the system that creates death into a new reality of life.

At the dawn of the sixties, Baldwin is convinced that nephew James must choose the moral high ground and accept white Americans, "You must accept them and accept them with love, for these ... people have no other hope." Later his outlook would change considerably, after the collapse of the civil rights movement following King's assassination and the rise of Black Power. At this junction, though, Baldwin echoes Jesus when

he counsels occupied Jewish followers to love their enemies—
except in Baldwin's case, *I am the enemy* nephew James is being
counseled to love.

White Americans like myself, Baldwin says, "are still
trapped in a history that they do not understand; and until they
understand it, they cannot be released from it."[74] Baldwin is not
saying that James needs to love white people because he needs
something from them, whether love reciprocated back, societal advancement, or even necessary racial justice. That would
still give white people too much benefit of the doubt, too much
power to dictate love on our terms. Instead, Baldwin tells James
to love, even his white enemy, because he's convinced that our
liberation is bound up together and it is the only way to break
the cycle of violence.

It is easy to cheapen love or to use love as an optimistic,
glossy way of denying injustice. Baldwin hated false love and
spoke against it frequently. At the end of his book, *No Name in
the Street*, Baldwin is full of anger and trauma from the end of
the 1960s which saw seemingly every leader supporting racial
justice shot down, from Dr. King to Malcolm X and Robert
Kennedy. Baldwin is broken at that point and far less hopeful
about the prospect of white America to change, nor does he see
it as part of his vocation any longer to persuade us to change.
He's fed up, and understandably so. As scholar Eddie Glaude
puts it, summarizing Baldwin's outlook, "It is up *to white people*
to release themselves from their own captivity."[75] Yet Baldwin
never ceased believing in the transformational power of love.
Even Black Americans thoroughly crushed by racism in the
United States, he says, speak "out of the most passionate love,
hoping to make the kingdom new, to make it honorable and
worthy of life."[76]

For those white folks who might be reading, Baldwin provided piercing insight into the creation of racial identity. In his

earlier "My Dungeon Shook," he turned his analysis to whiteness, and how Black and white Americans' history and future
are yoked to one another. I find it both unifying and devastating:
"They have had to believe for many years, and for innumerable
reasons, that black men are inferior to white men…. The black
man has functioned in the white man's world as a fixed star, as
an immovable pillar: and as he moves out of his place, heaven
and earth are shaken to their foundations."[77]

As Black liberation becomes a more imminent reality,
Baldwin thinks that white people like me are faced with an identity crisis. From the beginning of the American project, there
has been no creation of "white" without ownership of "Black."
Whiteness is wed to Blackness in a lineage of terror. For white
people to begin to love ourselves, therefore, means to take off
the masks that hide us from our own brutality and to begin to
reckon with the violence that has been done in our names. This
identity crisis is really a conversion to the way of love. It shakes
us to our roots, and most would rather deny the truth or dig ever
further into hatred.

"We know love by this, that he laid down his life for us—and
we ought to lay down our lives for another," it says in that tiny,
over-looked book in the back of the Bible (1 John 3:16). The
writer was addressing a tight-knit, small, beleaguered community that was to be known by their radical love. A community
that would be inspired by the loving witness of Jesus, who—
rather than pick up arms against the Empire—demonstrated a
greater power. The power of love.

"Little children," the writer says as if writing to nieces
and nephews, "let us love, not in word or speech, but in truth
and action. How does God's love abide in anyone who has the
world's goods and sees a brother or sister in need and yet refuses
to help?" (1 John 3:17-8). How can white, American Christians
call ourselves loving if we do not love in truth and action, that

is, if we do not face the truth of our complicity in the economy of slavery and theft of Native lands and do what can to restore and repair justice? Love, for white people, is to face reality and begin to change it. When we do this, we will be free.

•   •   •

CELEBRATE ONENESS AND DIFFERENCE

What did the mystic say to the hot dog vendor? "Make me one with everything." Silly? Yes, but it captures a basic point. The old joke means: Mystics seek oneness.

People who chronicle the mystical life often use language of "union" to describe what they've only glimpsed. Evelyn Underhill says mysticism is "the art of union with Reality."[78] There's even a long tradition in Christian tradition of so-called "spousal mysticism." Sixteenth-century Spanish mystics like John of the Cross and Teresa of Avila found such delight in divine love that only ecstatic exclamations of erotic, marital union could approximate their experience. Mystics from early Christianity onwards read the erotic poetry of the Hebrew Bible (yes, it's in there!) and applied it to the soul and God: "I am my beloved and he is mine," says the poetic voice of the Song of Songs (6:3).

Anyone who cares about the world, or even their neighborhood, today is painfully aware how far we are from union. Our cultural, political, and moral landscapes are filled with wounded division, gross abuse of power, groupthink, vitriol, scapegoating of the different, and attribution of evil to the other. It's almost enough to give up on unity. What can the mystical vision of oneness possibly offer such a world? How can there be true oneness without justice for all, especially for those who suffer most? And if we take sides, say, with the poor or immigrant person, or the incarcerated person, or the transgender person, does that mean we are giving up on oneness because certain neighbors will be upset? If we are concerned about climate change, and advocate for policies that will bring upheaval to a fossil-fuel addicted economy, we are necessarily generating conflict, indeed a type of division rather than oneness, with the way things are. What's a compassionate, everyday mystic to do?

At a Center for Action and Contemplation (CAC) conference in 2010, Brian McLaren talked about three stages towards union, or "unitive consciousness." First, he said, there is naïve oneness, followed by duality, which then eventually gives way to a more mature and heterogeneous oneness.[79]

Naïve oneness, on the positive and innocent side, is the undifferentiated union of mother and baby in utero. But out of the womb, naïve oneness often takes a harmful turn: it's the narcissistic claim of the white, privileged person doing yogic breathing and heralding "oneness with the universe"—but with little to no awareness of systemic racism. Bible readers will recall the desired "one language" of the builders of Babel's tower, the imperial claim of powers to make the world in their image: "Look they are one people, and they all have one language, and this is only the beginning of what they will do" (Genesis 11:6). Instead of a oneness that values diversity, naïve oneness is the ego doing the self-preservation that the ego normally does. When naïve oneness meets institutional power and privilege, it clings to it all costs.

Duality and separation are a fact and not negative in themselves. We order our lives by binaries. Another frequent CAC presenter, Cynthia Bourgeault thinks our either-or thinking is a central part of our consciousness; it is the "egoic operating system."[80] For instance, I'm grateful for the code that wrote the program to build the computer on which I'm typing this book. And I drove to the grocery store today and made a binary, either-or choice to stop at the stop light when it turned red instead of crashing into the oncoming car. We necessarily differentiate from our parents in order to become our individual, adult selves. We are constantly choosing "this" and not "that," and that's good.

The holy and ordinary mystic is one who knows how to operate in a world of binaries but also sees that reality is always more than two. A consciousness that has moved beyond dualism understands and participates in a wide and inclusive reality beyond Black/white, male/female, LGBTQ+/straight, Christian/non-Christian, citizen/undocumented immigrant. Compassionate wholeness holds a consciousness that is more than dual or what some writers call *non*-dual.

Just what is such a nondual or "unitive" consciousness? It's far easier to name what it's not than to articulate what it is, but you know it when you see it. The elderly person with a unitive heart who has nothing to prove, shines authentic joy, and speaks with just as much sparkle to children as with adults. The person who awakens the passion of being alive within you and makes you laugh more than you thought possible. Union is when I hunker down by my local brook and the incessant gurgle and flow of water cracks open something spacious inside me. Nondual or "unitive" consciousness is the elusive oneness that emerges only after learning from and even loving duality and difference.

First-stage, naïve "oneness" is really another word for domination and homogeny. When white people in the United States nurse resentments and grievances against *those* people, it festers into white nationalism and supremacy. It is "oneness" only for the few. Mega-corporations who sell the world their products may seem to be bringing people together but the brand façade often hides the injustice of Babel all over again. The world uses Google to search the internet and Meta's Facebook and Instagram to share their lives—but whatever nondual consciousness is, it is more than that. Instead of homogeneity and echo-chamber scrolling, unitive consciousness is, paradoxically, a oneness the includes difference. It is the spacious ability to honor multiple truths and identities without falling prey to the postmodern trap that would have us believe that multiple truths and identities are all there is.

Jesus lays claim to a spiritual fact of unity when he says, "I and the Father are one" (John 10:30) and then prays "that they may all be one" (John 17:21). But Jesus also shows in his life and ministry that the oneness he experiences with the Father is anything but naïve. The oneness he experiences with the divine is the same oneness that he enacts with everyone around him—whether eating with tax collectors, healing lepers, hanging with the poor, or delivering the demon-possessed. "You will always have the poor with you," he tells his followers (John 12:8), not because he is insensitive to the pain of poverty, but because Jesus followers are the ones who are united with those who suffer.

The mature mystic understands that the excluded can make up a cast of saints rather than a deviation from the binary code. The degree of solidarity that one demonstrates with people who suffer mirrors the degree of growth in true unity.

·   ·   ·

FIND GOD AT THE MARGINS

The monks who produced Ireland's ninth century Book of
Kells, appreciated the pregnant possibility of margins. They
cherished the biblical text itself—and parts of it are reproduced
on those famously gorgeous pages—but what causes tourists to
line up in Trinity College Dublin's Library to see them is something else entirely. People peer into the glass display cases to see
the splendid color of ink illuminating letters, Celtic knots tying
Gospel text, the oldest Western image of the Virgin Mary, and
even hidden cats prowling amidst the first two Greek letters, or
"Chi-Roh," of Christ's name.

To pay attention to margins is to pay attention to how
boundary lines are constructed in our world and lives—and
then to cross those boundaries. The psyche draws boundaries around what it is willing to face, so exploring unconscious
desires through shadow work is a way of welcoming the Holy
Spirit into our inner margins.

For contemplatives to engage margins, especially contemplatives accustomed to the comfortable and majority center,
requires a heart's nimble resilience across social space. My own
experience befriending Boston's marginal homeless population
transformed my sight so I could see homeless people as beautiful
bearers of God's image. When I moved into a scrappy Catholic
Worker-inspired community called Haley House nearly twenty
years ago, twelve intentional community members operated a
soup kitchen from the brownstone building's first floor. Each
morning, I woke at 5:25 a.m. and in a stupor of sleep rushed to
the basement walk-in refrigerator to make breakfast for dozens
of men. With coffee brewing, I opened the doors for early arriv-
als, the men who had slept on the street in hidden corners and
were eager for a heated room.

One man went by the name Brother George. He often

stumbled in at 7 a.m. already drunk. George was a gentle soul. He drew pictures on the day's menu board of a cartoon, tie-wearing man. I didn't know what it meant, but it was George's signature. He waxed nostalgic about former days in the Ukraine. "I was a master barber!" he repeated with flourish, to anyone who would listen. Many of the men invented stories, but I liked to imagine George having his own barbershop, cracking jokes with customers as he gave them a hot shave. Sometimes George laid his head down on the table and wailed in grief. Sometimes he urinated in his pants. When this happened, the other homeless men sat two chairs away from him because of the stench.

I didn't change George or persuade him to stop drinking. I moved on and lost touch with George, and I suspect he has long since died, but seeing him day in and day out changed me: I recognized his intrinsic human beauty and tragedy. I somehow knew that my wholeness was bound up with his wholeness; my wounds connected to his wounds.

In sociological terminology, margins make up a fluid and even ambivalent sphere: marginal people live in the two worlds of both dominant and subordinate spaces of existence. Some wish they could escape margins and taste more of the center. George was a citizen in the world's most powerful and wealthy country, yet he slept on the streets and packed his belongings in a shopping cart.

Or, marginal life is often "over-against." A group at the periphery of a culture or society's center develops subcultures antithetical, even violent or offensive, to those in the center. Marginalized youth sometimes turn to a marginal drug economy because it seems to be the only employment available. Adults among the working poor sometimes disdain the rhetoric and policies of elite politicians on both left and right. They are "over and against" the center of power.[81]

Jesus is a pioneer of transformation at the margins. Once John the Baptizer dunks Jesus in Jordan's waters, Jesus heads immediately to the wilderness for Satan's testing. The wilderness in the Bible is a peripheral place of challenge and endurance where God stirs up transformation for those who desire it. Jesus faces demons of power, fame, and adulation, and it's only after nearly reaching for rocks as bread that he is freed to proclaim: "Repent, for the kingdom of heaven has come near" (Mark 1:15). Somehow testing, trials, and margins awaken us to God's nearness.

God loves the margins in Jewish and Christian tradition. You could say God colors in them. The ancient Israelite story is one of relationship with God through successive marginalized identities: first as enslaved brick-workers under the Egyptian empire, then as a liberated but nomadic people. Once landed, ancient Israel nevertheless suffers the marginal fate of a small nation sandwiched between rival imperial powers, vacillating in fealty to Babylonians and Assyrians. They eke out a thriving, if precarious, existence under King David and Solomon, only eventually to be crushed and exiled by armies directed by Nebuchadnezzar and Tiglath-Pileser III. The homeless, traumatized yearnings of exile then give birth to the tortured cries of Jeremiah's Lamentations, but also Isaiah's soaring visions of wholeness: the wolf shall lie down with the lamb, the cow and the bear shall graze.

Christianity's roots lie in the wilderness wandering, exiled testimonies of ancient Jewish people. But many people in my country still today believe that Christianity's proper place is at the center. Political advocates known as religious nationalists claim that America is a "Christian nation" while affirming a Christianity that is racist, violent, and reality-denying. In the shift to the center, Christianity's essence is killed.

But this is not new. The early Christian movement was first a marginal underground network that refused to fight in Roman armies, and included men and women, rich and poor, the enslaved and free (Galatians 3:28–29). Jesus stresses that "the poor you will always have with you" (Mark 14:7) because Jesus' grassroots movement *was made up of the poor.* This all changed when Emperor Constantine had a vision of the cross in the sky and Rome itself became Christian. Constantine ordered his troops to paint the two Greek letters (Chi-Roh) of Christ's name on their shields. Christianity went from a movement of peace to a religion blessing imperial war. Those Celtic monks illustrating the Book of Kells no doubt had something different in mind.

There are also those many Christians in historic denominations who long for the old days when pews were packed and young families flocked to church, when Christianity dwelled still in the center of American cultural life. The exodus of people from church who choose "none" of the major religions on religious affiliation surveys or who claim to be "done" with religion altogether have prompted panic and grief for those remaining in the Christian fold. This seismic change, however, is pregnant with transforming possibility. Something is dying, something is being born, and now is the time to rediscover the small but mighty love mobilization that Jesus began.

What the present moment may be asking us is to embrace the power and wisdom of the margins. For white people coming from privileged backgrounds, this may mean non-defensive, open-hearted listening to the marginalized life experiences of Black and brown Americans. Once hearts are cracked open, for example, to hear the horror of African American experiences, first of slavery and lynching, and now of incarceration, the war on drugs, and gun violence, it becomes a transformative human response to affirm racial justice with grief, prayer, solidarity and action. Once hearts are cracked open to hear and honor immigrant and refugee stories, our hearts become broken at America's long legacy of turning away or disenfranchising those who differ from the white mold. And once hearts

are broken, it ceases to become an ideology for people of privilege to stand with the marginalized. Solidarity with the different becomes simply a natural human response of compassion,
reflecting our inherent, yet fragmented, oneness.

Margins are where God colors and spends time, and margins are holy places beckoning us towards greater wholeness.
The margins of our communities do not need us to "save" them
but we do need to cherish margins in order to know who we are
and who God is.

•   •   •

SEE WHITENESS

If you are white and you don't yet see it, please do something to
change that. Maybe even these words will help. Whiteness is a
system of privilege that I blended into easily but took me a long
time to see. I grew up poor, even though I didn't know it at the
time. My dad took a pastoral job at the Congregational church
in a tiny farming town in Michigan. He earned $13,000 a year
for a family of four, but we made do. We lived in the church par-
sonage, gratefully drank milk given by local dairy farmers, the
occasional game gifted by hunters, and vegetables we grew in
the garden. I never thought of myself as having white privilege
because there were many privileges I went without.

But I could pretend to be less broke than I was. I could pass
as elite because I was white. It was also difficult to see my whiteness because I never felt superior to people of another color.
Then again, I didn't know many people of color, either.

I inadvertently joined a system of racism called "whiteness." I didn't do anything wrong. My intentions were good,
and yet by being born white in America, I unwittingly participated (and still do) in a racial identity that has blood on its
hands. Race is not biologically real, meaning at the DNA level,
we are all the same. It's now scientifically established that we all
come from Africa.[82] But race is *structurally real,* given body in economic, legal, and political decisions from early America, which
means that race was created.

Whiteness is the elusive elephant in the room. It's everywhere so we are able to pretend it's nowhere. For those caught
in its myth, it is difficult to see, and yet once we see, it's impossible not to.

In Mark's gospel, Jesus dialogues with a rich young man
and tells him that if he seeks entry into the heavenly kingdom,
he must sell all his possessions (Mark 10:17–27).

The man asks, "Good Teacher, what must I do to inherit
eternal life?" He seeks to impress Jesus, to flatter him, and yet
even his question contains the trappings of privilege. The word
Mark uses for inherit is the Greek *kleronomeo,* which is connected
to inheritance, which is connected to land, as if eternal life is
something one buys and sells. But eternal life is not something
to be inherited, a parcel of land that the landowner received
from his father, who in his turn received it as an estate passed
down from his father. Eternal life is a life in which the future
heavenly age and present earthly age overlap with joy, grace,
and freedom.

White privilege and wealth in America work through inheritance, because slaves could not own property to accumulate
for future generations. They were property for white men's
future generations at the lost cost of their own. Today Black
men, scholar David Roediger writes, are imprisoned up to seven

times more than white men, and nearly one in three Black and
Latino children lives in poverty, compared to one in ten for
white children. Unemployment for Native Americans is triple
what it is for white people.[83]

It's difficult to see this. It's easy to tell ourselves that the
problem of racism doesn't concern us where *we* live, even when
the possibility of not being concerned is itself a function of
whiteness's power. Or, in contrast, progressive people like myself
and the good church people I've served often think that reading
books, familiarizing ourselves with unjust policies, and feeling
slightly guilty about it is tantamount to taking action. We pat
ourselves on the back for our "wokeness" without awakening
to any real urgency of change. This, too, is possible because of
whiteness. Whiteness is the option to enjoy privilege and choose
justice or not.

Jesus takes the man at his word, recognizes that he is an
earnest seeker, and lists off the commandments to follow. "You
know the commandments. You shall not murder. You shall not
commit adultery. You shall not steal" (10:19). It turns out that
the man has kept the commandments. The man is a good man.
He has not murdered anyone, has not committed adultery, has
not dishonored his father and mother. Mark's Jesus slips in one
commandment, however, that is not listed in Moses's ten commandments, and it is this: "Do not defraud" (10:19).

Why would Mark add an additional commandment to
Moses's already complete ten? Why would Mark's Jesus tell this
rich young man not to defraud other people? Perhaps Jesus is
homing in on that which holds the man's heart and body hos-
tage, which is the man's wealth, which more than likely was
accumulated by taking from the poor and defrauding others.
One rarely becomes a person of means in ancient Israel or the
U.S. without taking from someone. The reality of whiteness in
America is built on theft. Writer Ta Nehisi Coates puts it this

way: "When we think of white supremacy, we picture "Colored only signs" but we should picture pirate flags."[84]

The rich, young man in Mark's gospel insists that he has kept all of the commandments, and yet Jesus gives him one more. It's an exceedingly difficult command, a command that privileged interpreters have tried to avoid ever since: "Go, sell what you own, and give the money to the poor, then come follow me" (10:2) The young man has led a moral life, and he is likely a respectable and kind man, but he does not have what it takes to leave behind his possessions and to follow Jesus. Disciples James and John and Simon and Andrew have all left their fishing nets and livelihoods behind and joined the discipleship journey, but they did not have as much. The more we have, the more difficult it is to let it all go. The more we have, the more difficult it is to be free.

The tragedy of this story is that the rich young man is a non-disciple, a failed follower.[85] I'm hopeful enough in God's lavish grace that I might still be saved and live a just, loving, and connected life. But first I have to fit through the eye of the needle (10:25).

One response to Jesus' challenge, for people coming to see that they are white, is despair. In various activist spaces of people talking about whiteness, I have often experienced a mirroring of religious spaces in which we wallow in guilt and self-hatred. A holy ordinary life, however, does not begin in shame. It begins with the love that God always has for us. As rigorous as Mark's tale is, it is ultimately a tale about love. After the young man claims he has kept the commandments, Mark tells us that Jesus looks at him and loves him (10:21). Jesus loves the man, gazes at him with compassionate intensity, and from that place gives the command that will set the man free. It's out of love that Jesus gives the invitation, it's out of love that we face the truth, and it's out of love that we respond.

We have much to overcome. In the nineteenth century, theologians and preachers engaged a battle of creation myths. On one hand was God's beautiful creation of all people and all colors, and on the other, humanity's twisted creation of racial hierarchy and domination. Christian owners of slaves needed to defend their right to own dark-skinned people as property, as less than men and women, as less than God's beautiful creations. One way they persuaded themselves they could be Christians while owning slaves was to come up with a false and terrorizing creation myth, a distorted creation story to fit their racism.[86]

They said humanity doesn't derive from Adam and Eve as one unified line. They traced our lineage instead to Noah and his sons. Shem, Ham, and Japheth are famous for a truly bizarre story in which Noah becomes drunk and falls asleep naked. His son Ham happens to stumble into Noah's tent while his father is sleeping and sees him naked. Apparently, seeing your father naked was cause for intense shame in that culture, because Noah wakes up, realizes what has happened, and instead of a cup of coffee and a hot shower, he issues a curse. He says: "Cursed be Canaan, lowest of slaves shall he be to his brothers" (Genesis 9:25).

In the minds of slaveholders, Noah's curse explained why it was God-ordained that white-skinned people were superior and therefore able to hold Black-skinned people as slaves. They thought: there it is, built into the natural God-ordained order of things. The Bible said it and they believed it, as if cursing Canaan and Ham meant cursing the Black or brown-skinned person. They used this horrific argument as esoteric proof text against the arguments of slavery-resisting abolitionists.[87] Such is the willful tragedy and violence against Black bodies in the United States, justified by a *false and terrorizing creation* myth.

In the beginning, darkness covered everything, and—as the poet James Weldon Johnson reminds us—God smiled at God's beautiful creation.[88] But slaveholders turned God's good creation story into a story of domination and unspeakable violence. Such a false and terrorizing creation myth is really the offspring of the destructive creation myth of whiteness. Whiteness is something white people too-rarely see, something that is often thought to be built into the structure of reality itself, but is really simply a creation. White people often don't think about having a race, but we make whiteness invisible at the peril of people of color and the souls of white folks, too.

White preachers and teachers could defend slavery and curse their Black fellow humans because of the legal, material dominance of this elusive reality called whiteness. Even today, these two creation myths, the story of Blackness's beauty and the story of white supremacy's terror, are locked in bitter struggle. They're not separate stories but intermingled.

.   .   .

EMBRACE LIGHT AND DARKNESS

In the beginning, God said, "Let there be light" (Genesis 1:3)—and there was. In the epic poem of Genesis 1, God demonstrates speech as a creative and universe-building power. God says "Let there be"—and the text repeatedly echoes "And it was so."

God in Genesis is a complex character: on the one hand, a king who speaks commands and cosmic building blocks jump to obey; on the other hand, and in between verses, a feminine presence. God is a spirit-wind hovering (1:2, in Hebrew, vibrating) presence over deep waters, a singer who before speaking words first sings masses of matter together. God is an artist who, after an inspired seven-day visit to the studio, takes a pause to stand back at her art—which is the universe—and assesses, "Very good. I'll take a day off."

God says, "Let there be light," and there it is, light. But our modern understanding of light is far removed from the light of Genesis 1. God here is separating out the light from the darkness, as if the two need to be split apart. At the very beginning, or at least the very beginning of Genesis, the text reveals that tired and old light-dark dualism. Light is good and holy, we're told, and darkness its opposite is not so good. Darkness is, we might infer, chaotic, scary and even evil.

Light in Genesis is not a sun, it's a spacious domain. The light of stars and planets, sun and moon, is not strewn across the sky until later (1:14). This first "Let there be light" opens onto a light that is still waiting to be populated with lights themselves. Light at this point is an artist's blank canvas entitled "light" and awaiting its color. But I want to follow courageous scholar Catherine Keller in peering more deeply into the verses to those places where light and darkness become mixed. Darkness becomes mysterious and alluring.[89] When God created the heavens and earth, the earth first was a formless void and darkness covered the face of the deep (Genesis 1:2).

Something is there in darkness—formless void—before God says the first word. But this formless void, whatever it is, sounds existentially terrifying. I'm not sure I'd like to visit it. Theologians and Bible readers have long derided this formless void as nothingness or chaos. But when God speaks in Genesis, it feels more like an ordered and understandable *something*.

Catherine Keller shows that paying attention to the original Hebrew offers us a lighter sensibility of dark, introduces us to a *tohu vabohu* where there would otherwise be formless void. Keller tells that that strange phrase from which "formless void" is translated—*tohu vabohu*—is sometimes rendered as topsy-turvy, nothingness, or hodgepodge.[90]

Come to think of it, an unformed hodgepodge sounds just about right to me. In spite of the Genesis writer's long outdated cosmology, the soupy mass a trillionth of a second after the Big Bang does seem to be a hodgepodge. In fact, astrophycisist and popular writer Neil Degrasse Tyson describes that unique post-Big Bang moment as "a seething soup of quarks, leptons, and their antimatter siblings, along with bosons."[91]

If we are to take Genesis at its word, we realize that this God does not speak or create from a kingly perch out of nothing. Something is there, first. God speaks from within and through the dark mystery, whether particles or the feminine Spirit hovering over waters. The mystery arranges itself: light and dark, together.

As an English major who eschewed studying science in college, I don't pretend to understand much at all about light. My cursory search for understanding obscures more than it reveals: Light is complicated and there are many kinds. There is the sun, of course, the source of our planet's energy. There is Cosmic Microwave Background light, which scientists say is the fuzzy glow leftover from the Big Bang. There is the field of optics, which paved the way for photography and eyeglasses.

Light is profoundly complex. For some reason, though, in spirituality we prefer our light to be simple. Light conquers the darkness and the darkness will not overcome it, John's gospel says (1:5). We lift up the light over the darkness, and then we praise the light and cast out the darkness. But Catherine Keller has coined a term that has stayed with me: "light supremacy," which sometimes brushes dangerously close to white supremacy.[92] In a system of light/white supremacy, darkness is no longer beautiful. The loving God who creates a very good world gives way to the white-master-god who speaks his command and expects unquestioned obedience.

Genesis is working its ancient wisdom on me, though, and I increasingly understand light and darkness as bound up together. It's from a pregnant, womb-like dark space that God says, "Let there be light." *Bohu* of *tohu vabohu* (formless void), Keller suggests, could even be related to a Canaanite goddess of the "primal night."[93] God separates light from darkness, but they both need each other. Both bear the breath of God.

Light is not supreme, even in the cosmos. People smarter than me are researching an unknown mass in the universe known as "dark matter." It makes up 85% of gravitational force in the universe, according to a description by NASA and the European Space Agency, and yet nobody quite understands what it is.[94] Sounds like a *tohu vobuhu*, or generative and formless void, to me. Contemplative teacher Barbara Holmes says of dark matter, "In a culture where darkness has been deemed a harbinger of evil, a marker of inferiority, the opposite of all things good and virtuous, the unveiling of dark matter holds out the possibility of communal 'conversion,' a rhetorical turning to hopeful things."[95]

Both light and darkness turn out to be far more than separated and simple. Light itself, existing on an electromagnetic spectrum, spans visibility and invisibility. There is light from the sun that we can see, including the light produced by our electricity, and there is light that we cannot see and is "dark" to us—whether gamma rays or ultraviolet rays.

"Let there be light," then, becomes more than pure light conquering evil darkness by divine fiat. Light and darkness are emergent processes born from and connected to each other. The two co-exist as separate and intimately together. To quote the psalmist, far ahead of their time, "darkness is as light to you, O God" (Psalm 139:12).

But as I suggested earlier, the Bible often perpetuates the light and dark dualism. Jesus is the light of the world, we're told in John's Gospel, the one who enlightens those who are in darkness (8:12). And the toxic brews of racism and science denial today make separating light from darkness dangerous.

The mystics, as usual, arrived there first. They always seem to have understood that light and darkness blur, and that the spiritual journey is to enter a "cloud of unknowing" or "dazzling darkness." That first phrase is the title of one of the greatest Christian mystical texts ever written; the second phrase originated with Christian medieval mystic Gregory of Nyssa. It seems to be far truer of our lives to admit that light and the darkness are bound up with one another. Spiritual transformation does not happen only on the light level. The inner work of facing the shadow, or repressed realities, of who we are, allows us to come to terms with both the beautiful and the bad. Some of our most painful experiences in life—whether heartbreak, illness, or death—often turn out to create a capacity in us for greater love. What we think is light shows up in what we think is darkness, and vice versa.

Spanish mystic John of the Cross endured and trusted this paradox. His fellow Carmelite friars imprisoned him for over a year. During that time, he tended his soul's spark by composing poetry. Against all odds, the experience of imprisonment enlarged his heart when it could easily have diminished it. He risked his life to escape; had he stayed he likely would have died in prison. He wrote:

> There in the lucky dark
> none to observe me,

darkness far and wide;

no sign for me to mark,

no other light my guide except for my heart—the

fire, the fire inside![96]

.   .   .

MAKE ROOM FOR THE HOLY

In a Bible passage often read at Christmas, the holy makes her embodied presence known in a tender visit between two expectant mothers, Mary and Elizabeth (Luke 1:39-45). During the Christmas holiday, the holy also makes her presence in the tender excitement we share with friends and family. The holy makes her presence known in an animal feeding trough, otherwise known as a manger (Luke 2:16), and in the uncorked wine and just-baked pies of a holiday feast. The holy makes her presence known in fields at night to bleary-eyed shepherds (Luke 2:8-14), and for some who live in snowy climates like me, in snowball fights and kids wobbling for the first time on skis. The holy makes her presence known at Christmas, and all times, not only in abundant joy but in spite of angel-induced terror, and in the midst of our deepest fear, sorrow, and shame.

As a pastor, Christmas Eve always served as a peak religious and communal experience. Attendance tripled that of Easter in one of my congregations as people came out and brought friends and family to church. With candles lit and voices raised, I experienced the night of Christmas Eve often bursting with holiness. I'm not quite sure why this holiday struck such a meaningful chord in my community. Perhaps the death-defying drama of Easter is less approachable than the cuddly, cosmic glory of Mary's "yes" to God.

Christmas Eve is a wondrous and weighty night because it's when Christians ritually remind each other of the Mary-inspired task of bearing God. It's a question that lunges toward us every night of the year, but at Christmas we are perhaps more ready to hear it: Will you, too, give birth to God in your life? Will you, too, birth love in the world?

Shhhh… Listen…

Is that a baby's kick?

John the Baptist, leaps, no—the Greek says frolics—in mother Elizabeth's womb (Luke 1:41). I imagine Jesus, who always turns worlds upside down, responding with a somersault, much to Mary's discomfort.

The essence of Christmas is pregnant as God-breathed possibility in the midst of our festivities and failures, but Christmas is usually more than I prepare for and requires more space than I, as part of the overly-filled middle class, often have to give. That's why the ancient hymn sings out, of Mary, "Hail, space for the uncontained God."[97] God needs space to expand and contract, just as does the universe, and yet there's so little space to breathe in our days.

Christmas is about a baby, but it's also about the soul. Mary mirrors the soul's yes to God. Christmas is about the soul, but it's also about peace. Christmas is about peace, but not the comfortable peace of the privileged, or the sappy peace of holiday cards and church pageants, but peace as wholeness and healing of the seeds of violence. It's also about justice, and not justice cloaked as the authoritarian abuse of power, or justice as righteous license to tear down every group but your own, but justice as compassion enacted in protection for the poor and vulnerable, which we still must believe is possible.

Christmas is not ultimately about Christmas at all. It's

about the liberation that comes next. After all, once John and Jesus finish their in utero gymnastics, Mary sings a song, and as speaker Rob Bell suggests, it's more Rage Against the Machine than "Away in a Manger."[98] Mary magnifies God, and her heart exclaims: "He has brought down the powerful from their thrones, and lifted up the lowly, filled the hungry with good things, and sent the rich away empty" (Luke 1:52-3).

God as breath, or Spirit, hovered over chaotic waters in the beginning and created a world (Genesis 1:2). And yet God waits for us to birth Christ, as the poet Denise Levertov says, and we are free to accept or free to refuse, because choice is integral to humanness.[99] Even if we choose death.

Mary says, "Yes," and in saying "Yes" becomes the mother not only of Christ, but of all who say, "Yes" to birthing God. And yet Mary is not a caricature of a submissive woman, giving into the male God's wish for a son. That's not what happens. Mary is a revered mother and prophetess of Israel. Decades of commercialization and fears of embodiment turned this story into a trite tale about a woman who has a baby without having sex. But this reveals more about us than it does about Mary because Mary exercises full-fledged agency in her own right. She is a mother, yes, but she is also a fierce liberation leader in the Hebrew prophetic tradition of Moses, Miriam, and Isaiah.

The Holy Spirit will come upon her, Luke tells, but this is more than a winking nod towards divine-human impregnation (Luke 1:35). Luke's Greek verb for "to come upon" is used to describe the coming and going of people and things, such as ships, says scholar Elizabeth Johnson.[100] It is an active verb about how God lovingly moves, about how God is born, and about how we participate in God being born in the world. Mary's "let it be unto me according to your Word" is Mary allowing God's living Word to flow, move, and come upon her own life, as effusive praise, as love and justice, in her own time.

The Sikh human rights activist Valarie Kaur, in a 2016 viral video, implored Americans to "breathe and push" because "our darkness is not the darkness of the tomb, but the womb."[101] A great transition is underway, and this new birth occurs not only in our lives, and not only in Mary's life, but through the evolutionary unfolding of the universe itself. Spirited matter expands and contracts. God's momentous, uncontainable birth manifests in no less a space than existence.

John the gospel writer throws us under the waterfall of mystery. He says: "The Word was with God, and the Word was God in the beginning, and all things came into being through him" (1:1). A little later, John drops his zinger: this Word, that very same Word in the beginning, has now become flesh (1:14). The lofty word incarnation, from the Latin *caro* for flesh or meat, is a way of describing how God shows up, how reality and religion are not separate, and how Spirit is perpetually enfleshed.

John's gospel Word is a way of articulating something we all know but rarely utter aloud: that whatever of the holy is born on Christmas Eve has to be born on other nights as well. The only reason the holiday is holy is because we create the space to pay attention and allow it to be.

The same vital presence birthing the universe, which in Genesis speaks night and day and separates stars from sun, is the same vital presence pulsing within Mary, is the same vital presence arising in our hearts, is the same vital presence we desperately need to dream and enact a new future together. On such silent and holy nights, God the Mother initiates us as mothers, too.

*   *   *

embodiment

PRAY THROUGH YOUR BODY

I was taught to be afraid of my body. Bodies were dangerous, potential vehicles for the devil, because bodies might lead to sex. All expressions of sexuality were morally wrong unless you were married and heterosexual. But the messages were confusing, because my parents, youth pastors, and school teachers also taught me that my body was a temple of the Holy Spirit, that God had created it and called it "good."

My undergraduate alma mater is a small, evangelical Christian liberal arts college tucked away on the North Shore of Boston. I loved my time there and made some of the best friends of my life, and yet it was there that I struck upon further fear of bodies, my own and others. Each student signed a "Life and Conduct Statement" committing to refrain from sexual activity before marriage. It's a pretty standard, if unrealistic, evangelical college practice. But the statement singled out LGBTQ+ people, requiring such students to sign and pledge that they will not participate in "homosexual practice." Those who are afraid of LGBTQ+ bodies were perpetuating fear upon those very bodies. It must be disorienting and terrifying to be queer in an institution that says you are divinely disordered.

My denomination today, the United Church of Christ, ordained its first gay minister in 1972, long before most other denominations had identified LGBTQ+ equality as an issue over which to battle. And yet, as seemingly affirming of bodies as my mainline church, and friends and colleagues appear to be, I have a nagging feeling that we are usually terrified of bodies, too. We mostly ignore sexuality as a topic to be discussed, relegating it to a de facto realm outside of faith. But this is to leave one of the most critical aspects of our lives separate from our spirituality.

God and sexuality are inextricably linked—whether we are comfortable with it or not. Many of us are starving for a spirituality of the body that is more than "Don't do that."

Christians across the ideological spectrum are afraid of bodies. Christian fear of embodiment, and specifically sexuality, goes right back to the earliest Christians themselves. They picked up a strand of Plato's philosophy that said our access to the spiritual truths of the soul are contaminated by the body. The way to God, they said, is away from the body, towards heaven "up there," not through the body and towards heaven "right here."

Early theologians revealed a profound ambivalence about bodies. Origen of Alexandria is one of the most forward-thinking intellectuals of the early church, teaching a breathtaking and universal scope to God's love. But even he was plagued by Plato's dualism and hatred for the body. Origen thought that dwelling in bodies was like military bootcamp for the soul. Eventually with diligence and discipline the soul could leave the body far behind, but only after having struggled against the mighty floodwaters of sexual temptation. Mystics could take the higher roads of celibacy and prayer and taste union with God, but those lesser spiritual beings who succumbed to marriage and child-rearing would have to wait until the afterlife to experience God's full delights.

The apostle Paul is also a favored writer for those who prioritize spiritual flights of fancy over embodied reality. "Live by the Spirit," Paul says, "do not gratify the desires of the flesh" (Galatians 5:16). On first glance, Paul's binary categories of flesh and Spirit seem to fit right into a dualistic Platonic glove, locked in their all-too-familiar wrestling match. But the Jewish renegade Paul is up to more than simple denigration of bodies, and it all hinges around what he means by the term "flesh." "Flesh" or the Greek *sarx* in Paul's writings is not the same as body. They're two different words. Flesh is *sarx*; body is *soma*.[102] Paul speaks very highly of soma-body in other places, arguing for a resurrection from the dead that is not physically disembodied (1 Corinthians 15). Somehow, Paul believes, that when God restores creation through resurrection it will be the healing restoration of material reality, bodies, injustice, and the whole universe. Paul opposes the flesh to the Spirit, but Paul does not oppose the body to the spirit.

Flesh or *sarx* in the letter to the Galatians means the desires we have that are opposed to God. In all of us there is an existential struggle between spirit and flesh, a struggle between desire for God and desire for reality apart from God. Some of our desires lead to spiritual fruits such as love, joy, peace, patience, and kindness (Galatians 5:22–23). Some lead to destructive ways of living: jealousy, quarrels, factions, envy, anger (Galatians 5:19–21). *Sarx* is life alienated from God. Walter Wink describes *sarx* in Paul as "the self externalized and subjugated to the opinions of others."[103] When we are too nice and try to make everyone like us, or when we posture in public a different self than the one in private, or when we take our cues about what to think from the latest email from the Republican National Committee, the Democratic National Committee, or MoveOn.org, when we lock our suffering inside and pretend that everything is ok when it's not, we are living life according to the flesh. *Sarx* is not the body, it is the part of ourselves that is not free.

One way for Christians to overcome their fear of the body is to reread Scripture and rediscover the Jewish, this-worldly, life-affirming heartbeat of the Bible. But we also need to engage in practices of prayer that honor rather than devalue or ignore our bodies. Protestants like myself are far too heady, which itself is a way of dishonoring the body. The poet Edwin Muir wrote about Scottish Presbyterians that "the word made flesh here is made word again,"[104] and that pretty much sums up most Protestant worship services since the Reformation. And for those Christians who are unafraid to dance, raise their hands and pray for the sick, all too often they still combine their swaying songs with an anti-body theology.

Consider all the ways that you might reach out to God through your senses, most of all through touch. One practice that a friend recommended to me is, on a warm enough day, to go outside and hug a tree. Yes, be a tree hugger. And don't hug the tree for five seconds, do it for five to ten minutes. The tree's bark might be prickly and feel awkward. It might take a minute to overcome the initial self-consciousness. But when I've done this in my backyard, I linger with the tree, the tree lingers with me, and I eventually feel my body connected to the ground, to the tree, and to life.

Buddhists and yogis have much to teach Christians about the positive value of the body—as well as it's inevitable impermanence. Buddhist inspired mindfulness practices teach us to draw our attention to this moment, this breath, and this bodily sensation right now. I became a dedicated yoga practitioner because breathing and moving together intuitively felt like praying in my body. I didn't have the language or theology to articulate it at the time, but my body knew what I was doing was sacred.

Christians have work to do in order to knit prayer lives back together with bodies. Regardless of what form it takes, whether weeding the garden, walking mindfully, practicing yoga, or having sex with a loving and trusted partner, praying through our bodies reminds us that Spirit reveals itself through our bodies and not in spite of them. And really, how else could we pray other than through and with our bodies? Embodied prayer is an invitation to a transformed, Spirit-soaked rhythm of life.

*   *   *

GREET CHRIST LIKE A YOGI

I began practicing yoga many years ago, and it helped me overcome my fear of bodies. It awakened something very deep in me, which I hope to pass along to you.

Many people in the West have long been turning East to find spiritual meaning and discover what I've been calling the holy ordinary. From the Beatles and baby boomers taking up transcendental meditation, to D.T. Suzuki's influential spreading of Zen in America, to Sri Swami Satchidananda opening the Woodstock music festival, to Hindu ashrams sprouting in rural Pennsylvania and Western Massachusetts where I live, to yoga exploding in popularity so much that it is today offered at

your local YMCA, there has been a spiritual revolution underway of Westerners turning for wisdom to the East for over a
generation.

I probably wouldn't be a Christian today were it not for discovering yoga. I went through a long stretch of being bored with
church and Christianity, of not finding any substantive meaning
in what I said I believed. This crucible of faith also happened
to take place in the middle of my ordination process! I served as
a chaplain intern at a Boston hospital, enjoyed sponsorship for
ordination by a Boston church, but when my life encountered
crisis, the desire to worship and be with other Christians completely left me. It didn't feel meaningful. And I felt disconnected
from the deep grief I was carrying.

I found one place where I could experience an embodied
connection to the Holy Spirit, a place where I could be real
about my anger and sadness, and where I felt safe in allowing
tears to stream down my face. That was yoga class. And so,
on many Sunday mornings, I didn't tell anybody where I was
going or apologize to the minister. I just skipped church and
rolled out my yoga mat on the hardwood floor of Back Bay
Yoga studio in downtown Boston. I did downward dogs and
upward dogs and headstands and handstands and wheels and
cobras and camel poses. The irony is that as I created distance
from church, I found myself longing to belong more fully to my
Christian tradition. I started sitting in silence and reading books
about prayer and Christian mysticism. I went to a retreat on
the true and false self with Richard Rohr. I learned Centering
Prayer from Cynthia Bourgeault. I grew thirstier to know and
lead from within the depths of spiritual transformation that had
existed all along in my home tradition, but which no one in
church had ever told me was there.

Matthew the gospel writer turns East in a Bible passage
Christians associate with the holiday called Epiphany. The

Epiphany is intended to mean the revelation or "manifesta-tion" of Christ. Matthew writes about a group of people that I like to think of as the yogis of the day, known as Magi, com-ing to visit the newly born Jesus (Matthew 2). They were not Jewish, nor were they Christ-followers. They were astrologers, likely from Persia, known for dabbling in the supernatural. The word "magi" comes from the Greek word *magus*, from which we get "magic." Magi dwelled in king's courts, but they were not themselves kings. Some would have been philosopher-intellec-tual types, hanging out at the ancient equivalent of metaphys-ical bookstores. Some would have maintained esoteric beliefs such as providential revelation through stars. Some would have interpreted royal dreams. Some would have been snake-oil spiritual salesmen hawking cheap tricks. These are the people who Matthew tells us first witnessed and worshipped the infant Christ.

Matthew contrasts the response to Jesus between these for-eign magicians and Herod's religious-political establishment. Upon hearing of the Messiah's birth, Matthew says, Herod was troubled (Matthew 2:3), except it wasn't only Herod quak-ing at the arrival of a new insurgency from heaven, it was all Jerusalem with him. So Herod gathered the whole religious and political leadership together: the chief priests, scribes, their fam-ilies, the intellectual class, to determine where it was that this threat to Herod's power originated. The answer is right there in their scriptures and they should have seen this coming: "For out of you, Bethlehem, will come a leader who will shepherd my people Israel" (Matthew 2:6). But Herod and his yes men were too fearful that the new king from nowhere would disrupt their fragile, brutal grip on power. So Herod responded in the way that imperial power often responds to a threat, by fortifying his position, increasing surveillance and covert operations, and when all else fails, by unmitigated violence against the innocent.

Matthew's choice of Magi visiting Christ first is unsettling. Magi were demonized, ridiculed, and accused of all sorts of false behaviors. The Roman historian Tacitus called supernatural claims of magi nothing but absurdities, and Roman philosopher Pliny dedicated himself to refuting what he called "the fraudulent lies of the Magi."[105] We can easily hear echoes of contemporary false accusations that "poor people just want a handout" or "immigrants are stealing our jobs."

Early Christian interpretation of Matthew's gospel didn't treat the Magi any better. Theologian Justin Martyr foreshadowed conservative Christian fear of Eastern spirituality today by claiming this was a conversion story. The Magi, he said, left behind the evils of magic "upon turning to worship Christ." Clement of Alexandria heard in Matthew's story a rejection of astrology, and a simultaneous embrace of the one true and new star of Christ.[106] We can even detect in Matthew's story a tinge of ancient orientalism, which we would do well to remember in the midst of Western appropriation of Eastern spiritualities today. Matthew depicts a rather one-dimensional portrait of unnamed men from an unnamed location in the East who bear special powers and awareness of God's plans. The reality of Magi in Matthew's day was more complicated than that—just as yoga is more than chanting Hare Om at Woodstock.

Even still, it's these Gentile "others," these Eastern strangers—not Herod's court or the religious insiders—who understand the importance of Christ's birth. They're the ones who take the journey. They're the ones who follow the star. They're the ones who fall down and worship. They're the ones who rejoice. They're the ones who bring gifts of gold, frankincense, and myrrh.

The Magi represent those who are drawn to Christ but may be journeying outside traditional religious structures. American religion has broken as a new spiritual awakening erupts.

Everyone knows that spirituality is on the rise and religion is on the decline. The fastest growing religious demographic is those who don't identity with any religious affiliation.[107] Many people within and outside the church are finding supplemental, often Eastern-inflected, ways of nurturing their spirituality.

People are studying Buddhism, sitting in insight meditation, going to yoga, and incorporating mindfulness teachings. Ours is a new spiritual landscape, and we should welcome it all. Today's Magi have a lot to teach us. One gift that an inclusive path of everyday mysticism can offer is permission and blessing for spiritual journeying in different directions. A holy, ordinary life in God can include the freedom to draw inspiration from other spiritual streams.

In the yoga pose *savasana*, also known as "corpse pose," the practitioner lies completely still for several minutes or longer. On a given morning, I can be found at 6am, before the kids wake up, my legs stretched out and my arms relaxed at my side. My breath slows and I allow the ground to support me. I often cover myself with a blanket. At least for these sacred minutes, I let go of the tension and worry that my body is carrying. I'm enough. Christ is closer to me than my breath.

.   .   .

CREATE SACRED SPACE

At fourteen years old, I visited the ecumenical monastery Taizé in Cluny, France. My dad and I drove there from our house outside of Geneva, Switzerland, for a spiritual getaway. The phrase "contemplative spirituality" meant nothing to me, and for all

I knew, a monastery might as well have been a synonym for a UFO sighting. I still identified as an evangelical Christian, even though many nascent doubts stirred in me about whether God loved me and whether God was trustworthy at all.

Picking up a thick and worn songbook from a stack, I sat on a meditation pillow in the midst of the vast hall. I don't remember what it looked like; so many people crowded the place that I couldn't see from whom or where the music originated. It didn't matter. Unlike the guitar-led praise songs with which I associated worship, these songs didn't have a pep-rally style leader energizing us. No one person led the singing—we all did. The tones wafted over me, along with the chanting of thousands of other voices.

I experienced the repetitious phrases, "Bless the Lord, My Soul" as arrows of love from the divine heart to mine. Much of the songs were sung in other languages. This, too, did not matter. All of us sang the same language of the heart to God. I kneeled on the floor, hiding my tears of relief, not knowing how else to receive the undeniable, and undeniably loving, divine presence. It's a memory I will never forget, a promise that even though I would experience over ten years of depression, doubt, and deconstruction, God and I had an understanding. I had tasted the source of love.

The spiritual life takes place in space. I don't mean outer space, as in the universe beyond the Earth. I mean that we meet God and God meets with us in physical and communal space. How could it be otherwise? Contemplation is not only something we do on our own in the solitude of our hearts; it is also the encounter with the Holy through gathered people in particular places.

When we recognize and treat the spaces we inhabit as holy, we illuminate the sacred dimension of our ordinary lives. Regardless of whether we identify with a faith tradition or not, our hearts are often still stirred by beauty in churches, temples, or mosques. Sometimes it's the music, spoken word, and friendships made in such places through which holiness is conceived, and sometimes it's the places themselves. From refracted light through stained glass, to sprawling and multi-colored frescoes, to stripped-down and sparse Quaker meetinghouses, sacred spaces contain spiritual power to infuse our earthly days with heaven.

So-called "secular" spaces, such as museums, likewise serve as a congregating point for intentional, set-apart, "holy" space. I experience the nearby contemporary art museum as my regional cathedral and my local art-house cinema sometimes as church. They do not replace the gifts of scripture and sacrament, but they provide inclusive space for religious and non-religious alike to gather and ask ultimate questions of what matters. And I meet God there.

Sacred space in the Bible evolves, and its evolution goes from tent to building to bodies. The ancient Israelites first start meeting God in a tent, but then they chose a king, conquered territories, and erected a temple. They met God in an actual building and created a system of sacrifice and ritual laws to align with their desire to meet God in that building.

Jesus comes along and critiques the ways that his own religion's sacred building and leaders participate in the oppression of others. Then, Jesus—a Jew, let us not forget—in John's gospel claims to replace the temple through his own ministry and body. The apostle Paul (also a Jew) presses the message even further by writing to Jesus followers in Corinth and saying, "You are temples of the Holy Spirit" (1 Corinthians 6:19).

We begin by meeting God in tents, we eventually move onto temples, and we focus on meeting God in a saving figure—until we finally realize that we can meet with God everywhere.

Sacred space is first physical in the ancient Hebrew imagination. The psalmist cries out, "How lovely is your dwelling place, O Lord God!" (Psalm 84:10). For this Hebrew singer, God's dwelling place has four walls. The Lord's courts are not an ethereal or individualistic realm; they are the halls and walls of the Jerusalem temple. To meet God in all places we must meet God in one place.

God's space is so important in ancient Jewish religion that the Israelites created elaborate rules to govern the construction of God's house. Bible readers understandably skip over these passages, but they tell a truth. The book of Exodus starts with a divinely-inspired slave revolt following a showdown between God and Egypt's evil empire. Then the book spends the final third of its text chronicling precisely how the ancient tribe is to relate with God through physical space. The details are a bit of a slog, but they signify something profound.

The Israelites are instructed by God through Moses to create a holy place for their liberating God to dwell. The people are at that point nomads wandering in wilderness. Long before they worship in a temple, they encounter God in a traveling tabernacle or "Tent of Meeting." The function of this meeting tent is as it sounds: it is the place where God meets with the people through the intermediary high priest.

Holy objects populate this holy place, such as the ark of the covenant. Before Indiana Jones impressed the ark of the covenant onto our cultural imagination, Exodus 25 tells that this sacred box was to house the tablets of the Ten Commandments. Specific instructions ensue from God through Moses: the ark is to be constructed just so with a durable wood (acacia); it is to be of certain length, two and a half cubits (three and three-quarters feet long); it is to be overlaid with gold. Israel's welders are to fashion golden cherubim—mythical creatures combining "the strength, ferocity, and regalness of a lion with the flying capability of a bird and the higher reasoning of a human"[108]— on the ark's cover.

These mythical, lion-bird-human creatures face each other on the ark's cover with a mysterious gap between them called the mercy seat. This mercy seat, Exodus envisions, is the precise space in which God is said to dwell. Isn't it tantalizingly evocative that God offers to meet in an in-between, empty space? "There I shall meet with you," God says to Moses, "from above the mercy seat, from between the two cherubim" (Exodus 25:22). We witness in Exodus the evolution of an early religious tradition—the ancient Israelites have met with God through their representatives Moses and Aaron, but meeting with God once is not enough. Next, they figure out a way to continue to meet with God by building a house where God lives and a seat for the divine to sit.

At first glance, the Bible's intense fixation on temple building projects and interior decorations may seem silly or boring. There are pages of this stuff, and the late medieval Christian inventors of Gothic cathedrals took their inspiration from the same. I'm convinced, though, that deeper truths pulse through such verses. Space matters because God dwells in actual space, whether the gap between cherubim, the simple buildings of Taizé, the Eucharistic altar, the art-house cinema, or one's personal make-shift altar. God is not only out there. God is right here! And when it comes to awakening to God, the choice of materials makes a difference. Color lifts the heart or depresses the spirit and how we arrange our homes, conceive lighting, pick out furniture, choose paint, and create personal prayer corners all have spiritual capacity because space is sacred.

Jesus' arrival on the scene in the Jerusalem temple is outrageous, especially given this background of Jewish sacred space. More than the other gospel writers, John sees Jesus as replacing the temple with his own body. He is also launching an attack on the economic and political system of the Jerusalem temple, which is the action that sets in motion events that lead to his death. In John 3, Jesus fashions a whip of chords and starts overturning tables in the Temple and driving people out. Right before his dramatic outburst, Jesus threatened the institution itself: "Destroy this temple and in three days I will raise it up" (John 2:19).

The religious and political leaders hear Jesus' declaration as a revolutionary call, but John throws in an interpretive aside for readers, saying "But he was speaking of the temple of his body" (John 2:21). For Jesus, his own ministry and body is an alternative site to encounter God. In shocking fashion, he enacts the liberating realization that nothing stands in the way of experiencing God—not even a temple, church, or religious tradition!

The apostle Paul takes this theme of sacred space further. In his letter to Jesus-followers in Corinth, he asks, "Do you not know that your body is a temple of the Holy Spirit within you?" (1 Corinthians 6:19). We meet with God in temples, the person of Jesus is a sacred site, and yet we ourselves are also temples of the Holy Spirit. God sits down comfortably in the mercy seat of our own bodies. The Hindu-Christian theologian Raimon Panikkar put it this way: "We do not have to undertake painful pilgrimages to distant places to find the Divine. The treasure lies underneath our own house, just in our family, in ordinary life, in our beloved, ultimately in our own heart when our interiority has been cleansed of any particle of selfish dust."[109]

We don't need to go on far-flung spiritual pilgrimages to discover sacred space. Sometimes it can galvanize the inner quest to travel to sacred places, but the depth of our quest is measured by the quality of spiritual aliveness after we return. Everyday mystics living in the holy ordinary, after all, affirm that God is everywhere and that the whole earth is full of glory.

· · ·

SIT AT WISDOM'S FEET

After chanting a few Psalms each morning, I typically say the
Our Father and Hail Mary prayers. Most people who've sat
through a church service know the "Our Father, who art in
heaven" prayer, while the Hail Mary prayer is often relegated
only to Catholic devotion. I don't have an articulate "theology
of Mary" to share except to say that after praying to the Father
and Jesus for years, praying to Mary feels like it embodies bal-
ance: "Holy Mary, Mother of God, pray for us sinners now and
at the hour of our death."

After I pray to Mary, I begin to pray with ancestors in
faith, asking for their support and strength. I pray to Howard
Thurman and Thomas Merton, but most of the people I pray to
are women. I pray to Julian of Norwich, Hildegard of Bingen,
Teresa of Avila, and others through the centuries, until I reach
Mary Magdalene. As a parting gift at the conclusion of my time
as pastor, one of my former churches surprised me with a large
print of Mary Magdalene. I look up at her hanging framed on
my wall, and I ask her to encourage me with fearless devotion.
Somehow by praying to these female ancestors in faith, I'm
encouraged by God's feminine presence.

Many wise women have graced my life—my mother Jean,
my grandmother Margaret, church leaders beyond count—but
there's one woman who has impacted my spiritual life in a special way. She's my spiritual director of nearly twenty years, a
minister and chaplain beloved by many who has throughout the
years given me the profound gift of spiritual friendship.

Part of her wisdom's efficacy is born from the length of
our continuous spiritual direction together. By now, she knows
my predicable pitfalls, stuck places, and strengths. She has
witnessed my adult life trajectory, first entering her office as

a perfectionistic, not-so-evangelical-anymore Christian, then during the fracturing of a significant relationship, to my having kids and settling down in a place, to my dedicated pursuit of the contemplative path. She knows just the right mystic to recommend or poetry stanza to recite that touches the essence of my current life situation.

Even from a Zoom screen, she mirrors for me the divine gaze of compassion when I bring to her a heart knotted with worry and exhaustion. This woman doesn't solve anything—because, after all, that's not what spiritual directors do. Rather, she listens to the meaning behind my words and gently guides with wisely timed questions. Noting the monotony with which I am sharing about my prayer life, she turns the conversational tide: "Mark, where are you experiencing joy this month?" (It's clearly not in my contemplative practices, at least not this time!)

She is never didactic, and yet her wisdom teaches me about the expansiveness of the Christian tradition. Wisdom is not something to be possessed, I sense when I'm with her. Instead, she stewards wisdom as a free gift and passes it on. She regularly quotes back to me the Catholic Eucharistic prayer that never fails to jolt with its ancient directness: "In your mercy, God, keep us from sin and protect us from anxiety as we wait in joyful hope for the coming of our Savior, Jesus Christ." Why "protect us from anxiety?" The prayer's specific naming of my condition uncovers my heart.

She often recommends icons, especially contemporary interpretations of faith-based social-justice leaders. It is she who first showed me the Martin Luther King Jr., Dorothy Day, and Harvey Milk icons created by Franciscan friar Robert Lenz. She introduced me to the stunning "Mary, Mother of All Nations" icon by priest and artist William Hart McNichols. In it, a golden robed Mary holds her arms in an embrace around planet Earth.

Mary is a wise and cosmic woman, the icon seems to be saying, wrapping cultures, peoples, oceans, and atmosphere in loving compassion.

I leave spiritual direction and am again relieved to be seen and heard with such kind perception. I am lighthearted in the reminder that divine love extends to me, too. I am buoyed by a confidence that I am enfolded by centuries of like-spirited saints, sinners, and siblings in questing faith.

Wisdom in the book of Proverbs is a woman. In Proverbs chapter eight, Wisdom is not something to be studied, or even basic moral rules to be kept—as important as those are. She is a female teacher walking streets and crying out at city gates to "pay attention!" (Proverbs 8:1-4). I can imagine her calling to us amidst a Times Square-like chaos of branded, blinking signs and competing shopfronts. We scroll our devices while Wisdom shouts, "Wake up! My gleam lasts longer than jewels" (8:11). Her depth cannot be bought or sold. She speaks about justice and marvels at the beauty and wonder of the cosmos.

Similar to McNichols's "Mary, Mother of All Nations," Wisdom in Proverbs is a *cosmic, divine* woman. In Greek, Wisdom is the feminine *Sophia*, which in Proverbs' creation tale is a generative, divine power inviting passionate delight. She says, "Yahweh birthed me before birthing the universe" (Proverbs 8:22). Before mountains, hills, dust, dark matter, and cosmic microwave radiation, Wisdom was born. Full of rejoicing, she is there witnessing YHWH's ancient world-building. Yawheh creates, measures, and employs a primordial, cosmic leveler to mark foundations (8:27-29)—and Sophia-Wisdom is not sitting by serving lemonade to her contractor husband. She is a master workman herself (Proverbs 8:30), offering God the Father tips when he gets stuck.

We sometimes think of ordinary wisdom as the earned matriculation of life experience, but in the Hebrew Bible

Wisdom is a name for God. She is both a creative power, a guidance for justice and the moral bedrock for living a good life. In books such as Proverbs, the non-canonical (for Protestants) books the Wisdom of Sirach and the Wisdom of Solomon, and even aspects of Job and the Song of Songs, Wisdom is present at creation, descends from heaven, and takes up residence with us. She roams streets teaching about YHWH's realm, teaches disciples and invites them to take her peaceful yoke upon them (Sirach 51:23-27). She even invites her followers to eat the bread and drink the wine that she has herself mixed (Proverbs 9:2).

You could even say that Wisdom is like a female Jesus.

John's gospel envisions the Word of God with God in the beginning, paralleling Wisdom's birth (John 1). Matthew's Jesus echoes Wisdom's serene invitation to rest, "Come to me, all you who are weary and are carrying heavy burdens, and I will give you rest" (11:28-30). In Matthew's gospel Jesus even speaks as Wisdom Herself, saying, "Therefore, I [Wisdom] send you prophets and wise men and scribes, some of whom you will kill and crucify" (23:34).[110] Through Matthew's head-scratching statement, Jesus speaks in a universal voice claiming both to be the one sending and the one sent. The apostle Paul, for his part, understands the crucified Jesus as counter-cultural wisdom. Paul has a bit of fun turning Proverbs' categories upside down: "In the wisdom of God," Paul writes to the Corinthians, "the world did not know God through wisdom, God decided, but through the foolishness of our proclamation, to save those who believe" (1 Corinthians 1:21). Becoming a holy fool for Christ *is* Divine Wisdom. Wisdom becomes embodied in one person to reveal such holy foolishness in many people.

Wisdom matters.

She is creative, powerful, divine.

She is female, compassionate, ecological.

She is cosmic.

The sacred scope of Jesus Christ brings together matter and spirit, the holy ordinary with the extraordinary divine and vice versa. Richard Rohr captures Wisdom's presence when he exclaims that "The incarnation actually happened . . . with a moment that we now call the Big Bang."[111] Christ-Wisdom is the spiritual presence at the beginning of creation and ongoing through creation, the ever-more complex life emerging through the evolutionary process itself.

Christ-Wisdom helps us rediscover a spiritually vibrant cosmology. Throughout cultures and religions, cosmology is far more than a specific scientific discipline of studying the galaxies. It has to do with the way we understand our lives in light of the whole. In the past, faith ceded cosmos to the sciences—and then often rejected the sciences themselves. The result was a small and shrinking religion, and a small and diminishing Christ.

A living cosmology, suggests mystic-activist Matthew Fox, forms when the sciences, arts, and mysticism mingle. He describes cosmology as needing "all three elements [science, art, mysticism] to come alive: it is our joyful response (mysticism) to the awesome fact of our being in the universe (science) and our expression of that response by the art of our lives and citizenship (art)." [112] To affirm Christ-Wisdom is to affirm the awareness that the arts and the sciences stir in us that there is more and that it really is all connected. Both Christ and Wisdom are a way of talking about the divine presence in all things and through which all things participate.

Wisdom soars through planetary heights and yet I experience Her grounded presence powerfully through spiritual direction. Christ-Wisdom is embodied not only through Jesus, and not only through women, but in all who receive her.

My spiritual director asks me, "How is your soul this month?" And I hear the healing invitation of Divine Presence, wondering once again: "Are you tired? Worn out? Burned out? Get away with me and you'll recover your life. I'll show you how to take a real rest. Walk with me—watch how I do it. Learn the unforced rhythms of grace" (Matthew 11:28–30, translation *The Message*).

.   .   .

KNOW MORE THAN BOOKS

I love books. I mean I *love* them. I consider books my conversation partners. My bookshelves reach nearly to the ceiling and are packed full. I look at my bookshelves and have ongoing dialogues in my head and heart about the author's ideas and my own. Will I sound strange to you if I admit that books are my friends?

The college library near me is built by a famous architecture firm and has spacious windows opening onto mountains and trees. It's my favorite place in town, not only because of the modern design but because of what lies inside. Not to be too sentimental about it, but on a good day I park my car, stroll across the quad to a scene of clouds parting and hills rolling, and I'm filled with gratitude. The religion section is remarkable, and I return from each visit with an ambitious stack of books that I intend to read but cannot possibly finish. In preparation for this chapter, I emerged proudly from my visit with a couple of obscure books about the fifteenth-century medieval theologian, reformer, and mystic Jean Gerson.

I had the great pleasure of serving as a pastor in a college town with an intellectual crowd. Each Sunday sermon's preparation brought me sheer joy, because I knew that my love of books would be appreciated by my congregation's love of the same. We all valued continual learning, thoughtful reflection, and a critically engaged faith.

But after all my reading, and after all your reading, dear reader, if we only know about God and do not actually know God, then our spiritual task will have remained incomplete. Knowing about God engages the mind, and sometimes the heart, but knowing God sets the soul on fire. Rob Bell puts it this way, "There is knowledge about something, and then there is knowledge that comes from your experiences of that something. It's one thing to stand there in a lab coat with a clipboard, recording data about lips. It's another thing to be kissed."[113]

For Christians recovering from an overly rationalized faith, the mystical traditions can help heal wounds. Mysticism is a stream of the experiential, flowing from the hearts of those who knew and know God. It is the record of those who respond to God's baptismal declaration that we are indeed beloved sons and daughters. They seek what ultimately matters. As the Japanese haiku master Basho said, "I do not seek to follow in the footsteps of the men of old; I seek the things they sought."[114] Jean Gerson put it this way: Mysticism is "the experiential knowledge that comes from God through the embrace of unitive love."[115]

I am a student of mystics not because I am anything other than ordinary, but because I am a seeker of God. And I long to be kissed.

In fifteenth-century France, Jean Gerson rose to the heights of the Western intellectual world. He hailed from humble beginnings. His family had little money, and he lived in a tiny hamlet so insignificant that it doesn't exist anymore. He depended on receiving patronage from a wealthy and well-connected theologian. He diligently studied for eighteen years in Paris until the university awarded him their highest degree, its honored doctorate of theology. In that same year, they made him its chancellor.

Gerson became most known as a reformer. A fight broke out about how to recognize papal authority. There were two different popes vying for the holy seat, one in Avignon, France, and another in Rome. This period in history is known as the Great Western Schism. Parisian clergy threatened either to secede from and split the Catholic Church, or to reconcile it through an ecumenical council. Gerson brilliantly wove through ecclesiastical and political minefields. He argued for the necessity of a council's collective deliberation. It worked, at least for a while, and Gerson played a key role in what is known as the Council of Pisa. Bishops and cardinals from all over Europe traveled to the Pisa cathedral in Tuscany to hammer out a solution of how to get rid of both popes and end the schism.

Gerson became a powerful political figure and a respected theologian, and that's how the world has remembered him, when they have remembered him at all. Yet the overlooked aspect of his vocation is that this towering public figure and intellect made his spiritual home in the mystical tradition. He walked a nuanced path of passion for the life of the mind wed to God-centered love from the heart. A holy, ordinary life.

He almost burned out. Like many clergy today, he faced a crisis of faith and vocation after having battled in the trenches of the church's conflicts. He oozed frustration towards fellow clergy and academics in sermons. He remarked in 1399: "How many of them want to seem wise in their own eyes, how many want to be learned and erudite? And so they waste their time on superfluous matters."[116] I've been there! Many who have dedicated years or lives to church ministry or volunteer leadership can sympathize. Who cares about coffee hour and the Sunday flower arrangements when the earth is burning and true religion is all hands-on deck? Gerson left Paris and settled in a small church in Bruges, Belgium for two years, and then returned to Paris with new vigor and more focus.

His vision was the marriage of the mystical life with ordinary life. We often think of mysticism as esoteric and irrelevant for a life of action, but nothing could have been further from the truth for Gerson. He started writing in French rather than elite Latin. His first book after the burn-out was called *Mountain of Contemplation*. He wrote his reasons for a more experiential approach to faith: "Simple Christians who have firm faith in the goodness of God and love him ardently have more true wisdom than scholars who have no love or affection for God."[117]

Gerson started teaching his students the history of mystical theology, and offered a course on it, which is known as his book, *On Mystical Theology*. He chose the experience of encountering God's love, the knowledge of God that emerges from mysticism, as more important than intellectual theology.

It can be a temptation to confuse knowing about God with knowing God. Living among too many books, as I undoubtedly do, feeds this temptation. Unless we encounter the beating, passionate, life-affirming heart of God, all our knowledge about God will lack the depth of love that makes ordinary life holy and gives human experience meaning. A pile-up of books can convince us that we know more than we do, but to know God is ultimately for our knowledge to be undone by love every time.

.   .   .

MEET GOD IN THE ARTS

One of the benefits of living in western Massachusetts as I do is the art. Each summer, the rural and relatively quiet towns bustle with people. They come for the Williamstown Theater Festival, a summer theater program that holds sway with the New York scene. They come for MASS MocA, one of the largest contemporary art museums in the country, known for rousing bluegrass, rock, and experimental music festivals. They come for The Clark Art Institute, a leading art museum and research center that caters to an academic crowd, and for Tanglewood, the Boston Symphony Orchestra's summer home. And it's not only the New York and Boston wealthy who soak up the fun. Locals like me usher for free theater, picnic at free outdoor concerts, and meet up with friends at the festivals.

It only made sense, then, to combine summer worship at the church I led with summer art. I sought to counteract the summer attendance slump by adding the summer art scene to our worship. Each Sunday, we curated a service inspired by a performance, film, or exhibit. We shaped prayers, Scripture passages, sermons, and occasional post-church discussions around art. This experiment, which I called "Art and Soul," resulted in Sunday prayers quoting playwright William Inge, a two-part series on Van Gogh's struggle with Christianity, visionary photographs about environmental catastrophe from Senegal-based artist Fabrice Monteiro, and more. It worked. Instead of people taking off church in the summer, we created an energizing conversation and community to be a part of.

The more I have married my appreciation for art with my dedication to prayer and study of Scripture, the more creative my spiritual life has become. Prayer, like art, is now, as Matthew Fox describes, "a radical response to life." And God, for me, is no longer the dissatisfied dictator of my childhood—God *is* Creativity and the arts express God's passionate life.

After all, in the beginning, God *created* (Genesis 1:1). And whether birthing the universe, forming a people, or liberating the enslaved, much of what God does in the Bible is creative. There's something intrinsic to God that pulses with new possibility, which is to say that there's something inherently creative in the nature of whatever we mean when we talk about God.

In the Hebrew imagination, God's first creative act takes place through speech. God is a spoken-word poet constructing worlds. God says, "Let there be light," and there is light (Genesis 1:3). Then God crosses artistic genres, trying out sculpting and gardening, too (Genesis 2). God makes the heavens and the earth and shapes the first human from the dust. God breathes into the human's nostrils the breath of life, plants a garden in Eden, and makes fruitful trees grow.

As the story continues, so do God's creative experiments. After creating a cosmos in Genesis, God creates a people in the book of Exodus. God separates water from dry land at the Red Sea, allowing the Israelite people to flee their Egyptian enslavers, echoing the first creation (Exodus 14-15). Later, when the Babylonian Empire sends the people into exile, the prophet Isaiah views it as an opportunity for God to fashion a new creation, a fresh act of divine freedom: "From now on, I will tell you of new things.... They are created now, and not long ago" (Isaiah 48:6-7).

God's creativity echoes through the Bible.

John's gospel understands Christ—who also goes by "the Word—as creative, too: "In the beginning was the Word, and the Word was with God, and the Word was God, through him all things were made" (John 1:1). Christ the Word is present at creation, participating in the art-making that formed our world.

God is creative, Christ is creative, and the universe that God creates is creative. The Big Bang explodes and new possibilities expand. Something that does not exist begins to exist. Astronomer Adam Frank describes that original creative moment of the universe: "In the beginning, there was a single geometrical point containing all space, time, matter, and energy. This point did not sit in space. It was space. There was no inside and no outside. Then "it" happened. The point exploded and the universe began to expand."[118] Mennonite theologian Gordon Kaufman reads John's Gospel to mean: "In the beginning was creativity, and the creativity was with God, and the creativity was God."[119]

We might then expect that Christianity would follow this creative God to flourish in a relationship with creativity, through the arts. It has happened occasionally.

Medieval painting traditions memorably featured biblical scenes. Italian painter Giotto pictured the Raising of Lazarus, the Kiss of Judas, Jesus' Entry into Jerusalem, and more. Both Russian painter Andrei Rublev and Italian artist Masaccio dared to capture The Trinity in image. Flemish painter Jan van Eck took on The Annunciation as well as The Crucifixion and Last Judgment. Duccio painted the Madonna and Child, as did Giotto, Botticelli, Raphael, and more. Michelangelo famously sculpted David, along with painting the Sistine Chapel's Genesis ceiling scenes (Separation of Light from Darkness, Separation of the Earth from the Waters, The Creation of Adam and Eve, and more).

But just as often, Christians have shown little patience for creativity, pointing to those parts of the Bible that seem to speak against it. In fact, they lump much of it together as a negative denial of God that they called "idolatry." The ancient Israelites believed that God could not be represented by images, paintings, or sculptures. Even the attempt to represent God through creativity was blasphemous, and so what was art to one culture was abhorrent to Israel. "You must not make a carved image for yourself," God tells Moses and the ancient Israelites (Exodus 20:4), levelling a damning critique of Egyptian sacred objects. The prophet Isaiah sneers at the Babylonian, imperial gods: "Shall I bow down to a block of wood?" (Isaiah 44:19)? One South African theologian summarizes the ancient Israelites' belief: "God alone was holy, God alone had the power to create and redeem, and therefore whatever sacredness might be attached to the land, to the temple, or to other natural objects was not inherent but derived."[120]

The way that sacred art and images are used within the Christian faith mirrors this struggle. Take, for example, Eastern Orthodox Christians and Protestant Christians. Eastern Orthodox have believed for centuries that images and icons can reveal the presence of God. They point out that Jesus is the "image" or icon of the invisible God (Colossians 1:15). As part of their worship, they include painted pictures of Jesus, stories from the gospels, and saints of the church. If you have never been inside a church from one of the Orthodox traditions, you must visit and see for yourself what I am talking about. It can be stunning. The role of icons for Eastern Orthodox Christians is to be a sign of the presence of God.

On the other hand, Protestants became infamous for their passionate opposition to images in church. Perhaps the most dramatic example of this opposition is a radical strain of Lutherans who became iconoclastic—which translated from the Greek means "image destroyer." These image-destroying Christians tore down stained-glass windows and church paintings; they wielded hammers against statues of the Virgin Mary. They even fomented riots, such as one in Basel, Switzerland that resulted in throwing art into fire, tearing down statues, and painting over frescoes.

Christianity is conflicted about the arts, and never more so than through the false religious category of the sacred and secular. Holy, ordinary mystics who understand that heaven and earth are entwined do not recognize such a split. Like the angels in the prophet Isaiah's vision, we see one sacred reality and "The whole earth is full of God's glory" (Isaiah 6:30). Yet history is full of those who choose fearful rejection of this world over the joyful mystery of incarnation. For them, there's sacred art that deals with Christian themes, such as paintings of the Madonna and Child, or the music of Handel, and then there's the secular world where everything else resides.

Every time I walk through the industrial doors of MASS MoCA, though, it's as if I'm entering a cathedral. I've stared up at the Last Judgment frescoes that cover the ceiling of the Cathedral of Santa Maria del Fiore in Florence, Italy, but the 250,000 square feet of sprawling and spacious exhibitions at Mass MoCA in North Adams, Massachusetts still takes my breath away. Each new exhibition reconfigures the space, and I'm invited into new experiences, thoughts, and creative possibilities. While religious spaces often anticipate predictable piety and prayer, I experience MASS MoCA, and other contemporary art museums like it, as a raucous and unashamedly weird way to stumble into holiness.

On my most recent visit, I entered the darkly lit second floor exhibition "Like Magic," an exploration taken by ten artists to explore "technologies of magic." I imagined magic sounds performed from Diné composer Raven Chacon's musical scores that are written onto the wall. Each score is made up of his own notational language that includes things like nonmusical lines and dots and simple instructions (For breathing, and holding a tone as long as possible / while singing / while humming / while whistling / while hissing). I experienced the possibility of magical, spirit conjuring when I walked, foot in front of the other, into a pitch-black, tent-like installation on the same floor, with speakers broadcasting eerie sounds. Instead of finding a side chapel where guests light candles and incense before statues of saints, I exited the fabric-tent and discovered the floor of the hall lit up by luminous mail packages. Created by Iranian artist Gelare Khoshgozaran, the boxes spread on the floor are actual personal packages sent from Iran by Khoshgozaran's mother, which were then opened and inspected by the U.S. Customs. The artist repurposes the parcels as glowing, interconnected lanterns. They looked like candlelight, but they were more, and I prayed for peace in international relations just as I prayed for peace in my heart.

The theology of incarnation gives me hope that Christians might make new pathways to celebrate the creative arts and experience God through the five senses in ways that art fosters. Contemporary art won't be for everybody, but the arts are an expansive umbrella under which everyone can find a place.

God is revealed through all things. This means God is not only present in the stereotypically beautiful or pretty, but also in tragedy and pain. Art that moves beyond Renaissance paintings and Handel's oratorios—even and especially art that expresses stormier emotions and disrupts staid certainties—can be put to godly use too. Maybe God's beauty is different from our own and itself *contains* the tragic, absurd, and agonizing. As theologian Karl Barth said, "God's beauty embraces death as well as life, fear as well as joy, what we might call ugly as well as what we might call the beautiful."[121]

The incarnation of Jesus unleashes the incarnation of reality: if the creative God has incarnated divine self in human, material life through Jesus, then human and material life are divine. And if human and material life are inherently and divine, then there is no separation between sacred and secular.

All of life is sacred, and to call a part of reality "secular" is simply a failure to appreciate reality.

The arts are an invitation to encounter God's creative presence in reality, which is to say that we find God in the holy ordinary. We meet God in the death, life, fear, joy, ugliness, and beauty of our own lives and world.

*   *   *

transformations

BE HAPPY WITH ENOUGH

The world is always luring us to crave more. The culture of "more" is a culture of not enough, accumulation and conquest, and sought but constantly deferred satiety. Every time we text message or update Instagram, researchers tell us that our brains loop in a dopamine cycle of neurological yearning.

We seem unable to discern when enough really is enough. From shopping to Netflix binge-watching, sexual hook-up culture to alcoholism, and the reckless gambling of Wall Street speculators, we are in thrall to both trivial and life-threatening addictions. Intervention in desire's consumptive assault is then written off as bad economics or puritanical repression. The very fear of limiting desire reveals how out of control desire is, and how, in fact, our excess longing imperils the planet.

For example, the Intergovernmental Panel on Climate Change has stated consistently for nearly three decades that human activities increase greenhouse gas emissions. Our crisis moment, however, finds Americans regressively debating whether climate change is a hoax while oil companies scour and drill Earth for more "exploration and production."

I am myself implicated in "more," a disease that Clive Hamilton and Richard Denniss memorably called *Affluenza* in their book of the same name, subtitled: *When Too Much is Never Enough*. This is because I live in the United States, the great purveyor of the myth of more, where my family and I are nestled in a beautiful corner of Massachusetts. There are lies, I'm sure, that I have told myself, inculcated in the culture of more, which range from the substantial to the mundane. If I work harder, my church/employer/business/family will be more successful and we will flourish. If I purchase more books, I'll acquire more knowledge and wisdom. If I drink another beer, I'll feel more relaxed. If I obtain that new thing, I'll be happy.

The desire for *more*, though, is a crisis of desire. What is it that we desire when we desire more? It's usually not the thing itself—whether a lover, job position, third-quarter earnings goal, or new style of jeans. These things fade away in desire's fickle dissatisfaction.

Seekers on transformation's path have known for millennia that desire's incompletion points inexorably to spirituality. A vibrant sacred-pursuing life requires a redirection of our longings to that for which we *truly* are longing. As the Catholic writer Ronald Rolheiser puts it, "There is within us a fundamental dis-ease, an unquenchable fire that renders us incapable, in this life, of ever coming to full peace…Spirituality is ultimately what we do with that desire."[122]

Another Catholic writer from a much earlier time, Spanish Carmelite mystic John of the Cross is a spiritual director for our obsessive age of more. He is known for his understanding of the "dark night of the soul"—those periods of faith in which our certainties, hopes for the future, beliefs about God, and even faith itself are eclipsed. But he also wrote about another dark, albeit less popular, night: the dark night of sense.

The dark night of sense precedes the dark night of the soul

in that it harnesses our desire and prepares our will to be ready to receive, meet, and fall in love with God. There is no union with God, John of the Cross says, without first curbing our appetites. No loving transformation without first setting limits. He poetically affirms that the goal of the spiritual life is love-drenched union with God, but today he might clarify that union doesn't happen first in yoga class, on a beach at sunset, or hands raised in a particularly affecting religious service. According to John of the Cross, union is instead the fruit of long, dark nights. Union is a gift after the sometimes excruciating process of detaching our desires from all that is not God.

Not everyone is ready for this, or able to undergo it.

This is why John of the Cross's book *The Ascent to Mount Carmel* doesn't fly off bookstore shelves. This teaching insists on a torturous-sounding process called mortification. This is one of those crusty, cringe-inducing words from mystical tradition that contains spiritual power but is widely misunderstood. And since the word is misunderstood, it is rarely used. Mortification, in theory, might sound like punishment in prison, but mortification in practice looks surprisingly like liberation.

"Mortification" is connected etymologically and spiritually to death. John of the Cross writes, "The mortification of the appetites can be called a night for the soul. [Because] to deprive oneself of the gratification of the appetites in all things is like living in darkness."[123] He is describing the often-painful process of letting go of the ultimacy that our appetites ascribe to non-ultimate people, places, emotions, substances, and things. Spiritual transformation leads through darkness because the process of limiting desires can feel like death. Just ask any serious caffeine addict who tried to give up coffee. Or talk to a person in recovery.

Anyone who is paying attention to global crises, however, knows that the opposite is true. It's not limited (mortified) but unchecked desire that leads to death. Death is on prime-time display in the form of irreversible climate change, deforestation, inequality between rich and poor, Global North obesity vis-à-vis Global South food insecurity, devaluing and over-sexualization of women's bodies, piling up trash in landfills and oceans, species extinction, and more. There must be a point at which we say, "Enough!" Mortification.

To suggest that appetites are somehow at the root of our problems and must be restrained is never a popular message. Liberals fear limiting desire because their sense of freedom is tied up in individual autonomy. Conservatives more easily set boundaries around personal desire but at the cost of valuing bodies, sexuality, and desire.

According to John of the Cross, however, bodies and desires are not the primary cause of suffering. It is critically important to say—in the context of a Christianity that has ignored, demeaned, and often abused bodies—that bodies are beautiful, sexuality is wonderful, and desire itself is holy. Rather, it's our wills that are the problem. Here's how John puts it: "The less strongly the will is fixed on God, and the more dependent it is on creatures, the more...the passions [inordinate desires] combat the soul and reign in it."[124] Our wills attach to the objects of our appetites, and we invest them with meaning and purpose rather than God. This is a basic enough movement of the heart, but it leads to spiritual disaster.

To give a trite example: I'm a compulsive email-checker. I intend, without success, to create boundaries around my phone. On any given day and in spite of spiritual practice, my center of emotional gravity is inevitably thrown off. I realize—usually after the fact—that my phone has become an extension of my hand and consciousness.

For what am I hoping? Sometimes it's for someone to write me back and sometimes it is an ambiguous, objectless sense of unease. I don't *know* what I'm hoping for in that moment, but I pull out my phone to provide a fleeting respite of relief from vague, ill-defined discomfort.

Mystics and theologians from Augustine to John of the Cross call this dissatisfaction "inordinate desire." This is the type of yearning within us that aches for union with the infinite but settles instead for the finite and thus perpetually lets us down. Sometimes it's as simple as the vague anxiety after checking email or notifications. Sometimes it's bland *ennui* or soul-numbing depression.

To heal unaccountable desire requires contemplative soul work. We find healing not in libertinism or repression but in identifying human desire within a larger economy of *divine desire*. Much of the work of Anglican theologian Sarah Coakley locates itself at this very intersection of contemplation and desire. Commenting on sexuality and gender battles in the church, she writes, "The current crisis is about the failure, in this Web-induced culture of instantly commodified desire, to submit all of our desires to the test of divine longing."[125]

The biblical writers said the same: "We love because God first loved us" (1 John 4:19). Ephesians chapter two does not end with Gordon Gecko or the Mall of America but in God's love for us: "God, who is rich in mercy, out of the great love with which he loved us…made us alive together with Christ-by grace you have been saved" (2:4-5).

All these examples point to desire of a different order: it's not excessive desire that leads to death; it's divine desire that leads to love. What do you need—really? There is Presence within the universe, a Christian faith affirms, that moves towards us with love. Those seeking a vibrant life in God welcome this love at their own risk, however, because it is fierce. It contains the trans-formational capacity to disrupt and realign our desires. The process is mortifying, a true dark night of sense, but worth the wait. Rightly ordered desire frees us to live lives that embody the wholeness for which our world groans, lives centered on mercy, peace, and compassion rather than consumption.

This is why a renewed asceticism is needed for a holy, ordinary spirituality today. We don't need asceticism that scorns the body or shames desire, but we need asceticism that affirms bodies and selves, while purifying the will so that our desires align with God's. We'll never be satisfied with gadgets, accolades, and more stuff, but the alignment of human desire with divine desire *is* the goal of our longing. As one of my teachers, James Finley, says, "The architect of our hearts has made our hearts in such a way that nothing less than an infinite union with infinite love will do."[126]

Infinite love is the intervention to the greed-fueled, desire-addled world in which we find ourselves. Wholeness and union follow the dark night.

•   •   •

ENTER THAT DARK NIGHT

"So dark the night!... I went with no one knowing upon a lover's quest—Ah, the sheer grace!—so blest, my eager heart with love aflame and glowing," sings John of the Cross, whom you just met in the section before this one. Now, I hope you are ready to enter in.

He's not the only poet or prophet who has conjured a dark night to describe the potent place between disaster and possibility. The poet Dante Alighieri opened his classic *Divine Comedy*, "In the middle of the journey of our life, I came to myself, in a

dark wood, where the direct way was lost." The Hebrew prophet
Jonah finds himself in a dark and stormy night at sea. His only
recourse is to give himself fully to despair and ask his fellow
sailors to throw him overboard (Jonah 1:12). In every instance,
the dark night is evocative, terrifying, yet meaningful, and still
containing unexpected sources of light.

Some have described our social and political crises as a collective dark night in which the brightness of justice and peace
have eclipsed. I remember early in the Trump presidency when
Immigration and Customs Enforcement agents raided undocumented immigrant houses in the middle of the night, many
Americans felt fear and instability. At other times during those
years, we experienced a President sending unhinged tweets at
night. During those days, too, women shared their #MeToo
sexual abuse stories, revealing that men's most harmful behavior often took place at night. If you are Black in America, dark
night is still not safe. I'm putting finishing touches on this book
during the hottest summer temperatures that have ever been
recorded on our planet. If the coming instability and suffering
due to climate change are a dark night, it is a scorching one.

So John of the Cross and his dark night may come across as
austere and difficult to connect with, as if he might be awkward
at dinner parties, an eccentric mystic that we admire but do not
wish to know—but this teaching also feels strangely timely and
relevant for our times.

John is a man wildly in love with God who pictures the
divine as a living flame of love that sets us on fire with love,
too. But he's not known for the living flame of love—he's
known for the dark night. He lived as a Carmelite friar in an
era of Catholic repression and renewal, the time known as the
Counter-Reformation. His religious order traces roots back to
cave-dwelling mystics in Jerusalem and to the Old Testament
prophet Elijah. John is friends with the famous mystic Teresa

of Avila, and he joins her as a co-reformer of a new Carmelite order called the Discalced or "Barefoot" Carmelites.

As joy and love-drenched as he was, though, some of John's Carmelite brothers thought he was pushing change too fast. Some thought Teresa and he were amassing too much power, and not everyone wanted to follow God with such passion and abandon. One night his own religious brothers kidnapped him, brought him to a town called Toledo, and threw him into a tiny cell. John lingered there in the dark for eight months until his escape. Under the protective cover of night, he found a way to fit through the small window in his cell and run for it.

The way that John survived his trauma was to compose poetry about the soul's dark night. Strangely, he does not describe his night as a night of suffering and torment, even though he has every reason to do so. Instead, he calls his night a lover's journey into the dark mystery of God. Such language needs to be heard to be believed.

The biblical prophet Jonah experienced a dark night, too. He flees God's presence and his own vocation and ends up in a fish's belly. He receives a clear divine call to a thankless mission. He is to preach a troubling message to Nineveh, the capital of the Assyrian Empire, confronting them with their own wickedness and warning them that their injustice will bring about their downfall. Like climate activist Greta Thunberg accusing international diplomats of more "Blah, blah, blah," Jonah's prophetic task requires the telling uncomfortable truths to the powerful. And he's not ready for that.

Jonah runs and sails in the opposite direction on a ship, but even in the deep waters, it turns out that he cannot flee God. Rain starts pouring and waves start thrashing, and God is the one stirring the storm. After some spiritual sleuthing to figure out why the seas are set against them, the sailors take up

Jonah's own suggestion to throw him overboard, where a giant fish (which tradition has called a whale) swallows him up. He remains in the fish's belly alive for three days and nights, and readers of Jesus' story are intended to take note. Dark nights do not stay dark forever.

I can't imagine Jonah could see anything in the fish's belly. He would have heard the crashes of waves and billows, or maybe the unsettling gurgle of giant internal fish organs pumping. I also wonder how he breathed, but we're not meant to poke literally at such tales. We are meant to understand that when Jonah has nowhere else to turn, when he's stuck in the dark and dank fish's belly, he prays just as we do when catastrophe buckles our knees: "I called to the Lord out of my distress and he answered me. Out of the belly of Sheol I cried, and you heard my voice" (Jonah 2:2). Sheol is the Hebrew term for the underworld, the place in ancient Judaism where souls left bodies after death, and Jonah is dwelling in the in-between.

Simply put, darkness is the place we most encounter God. Jonah and John of the Cross meet God in the darkness and the deep, even as God doesn't take away their suffering. John memorized his stanzas and called his dark night a lover's quest while he was still imprisoned. He's not saying that he loves being imprisoned, but it's because he's imprisoned that he has nowhere else to turn. In desperation, he stumbles into sheer grace. Where many would have met despair, he found love instead. For his part, Jonah claims that God hears his prayer not after the fish spews him out on dry land, but before. Redemption is not a false promise that it will all become easier, even if it eventually does. Somehow our relationship with God deepens in the darkness in a way that would not have taken place any other way.

Those familiar with the Jesus story recognize in John and Jonah a familiar pattern. To the religious leaders who are con- flict-avoidant and satisfied with feel-good religion, Jesus says,

"No sign will be given to you except for the sign of Jonah" (Matthew 12:39). What is that sign? It's three days and three nights in the belly of the whale. Or, as Christians put it, three days from the harrowing crucifixion to ebullient resurrection, also known as the holy "Triduum" or three-day journey from Good Friday to Easter.

We can even hear in John's dark night an echo of an ancient Christian hymn sung on the night before Easter morning. Christ rises before dawn in the dark, but it's a glimmering dark because "This is the night when Jesus Christ broke the chains of death and rose triumphant from the grave." Then the hymn sings, "Night truly is blessed when heaven is wedded to earth and humanity is reconciled to God."[127]

As much as we might prefer otherwise, night is the place when new possibilities emerge. To affirm such hope is not a way of denying the night's terrors. Instead, it is at its root an invitation for our hearts to be set aflame with love.

.   .   .

WELCOME CHRIST'S ARRIVAL (LIKE SHAKERS)

America's homegrown mystics, in little towns like New Lebanon, New York, and Hancock, Massachusetts, the Shakers planted vital outposts of utopia close to where I live. Their spirituality branched off from mainstream Protestants, prioritizing direct experience of God over-against dogma and religious institutions. Ecstatic worship, mixed with communitarian living and pacifism, did not make them many friends in traditional Protestant circles.

Our conversations about mystics do not typically include the Shakers, but they are perhaps one of America's greatest and most interesting contributions to the larger mystical cloud of witnesses.

I did what I could to infuse the Congregationalist church I served in Massachusetts with an appreciation of the Shakers' unique witness. We once held a Shaker-inspired service. With help from a staff member of the Hancock Shaker Village, we danced a Shaker dance, sang Shaker songs, and learned about Shaker history and worship. I sought not only to educate my congregation in Shaker ways, but to have us experientially taste the vitality of Shaker spirituality.

For them, Christ was not only coming in the future, Christ had already arrived. They first named themselves, clunkily, the United Society of Believers in Christ's Second Appearing. They shaped their communal existence by this belief in the "Second Appearing."

The tale starts with "Mother" Ann Lee in early eighteenth century in Manchester, England. She was one of eight children, born in poverty to a blacksmith father. In the middle of the 1700s, she becomes involved with a renegade Quaker group called Shakers, or "Shaking Quakers." Convinced that Jesus' second coming was imminent, these proto-Pentecostals were so full of the Spirit in their meetings that they shook, spoke in strange languages, saw visions, and danced.[128]

Pretty soon, Ann Lee joins with other Shakers in her small town to publicly proclaim that Jesus is coming back. Such world-changing news must be shared, they think, which leads Ann and her compatriots to interrupt a local church service to announce their belief. They are charged with disturbing the peace and thrown in the local jail. While sitting behind bars, she has an experience of Christ's presence. She envisions herself born again into a new life of complete spiritual renewal. It's such a transformational experience for her that she sees it as nothing less than the Second Coming of Christ.

Ann Lee begins speaking about her prison-awakening to other people and the message spreads. As she tells her story they, too, have a similar experience of the heavens opening and of Christ returning. Through Ann, their hearts turn to Christ's arriving presence within and through them, and they are initiated into (for them) the culminating event of history.

The Congregationalist establishment gatekeepers adamantly opposed this new, mystical sect. Planting roots across the state line in New Lebanon, New York, Massachusetts Congregationalists called Mother Ann a witch, harlot, and heretic—epithets that Puritans often threw at people they did not understand. The Shaker practices of celibacy, gender equality, and pacifism subverted Congregationalist religious status quo. The Congregationalists ominously called the Shakers a threat to the very foundation of society, which seems ludicrous but in a way was true. The Shakers threatened the established societal order by their very existence. Their communal, non-procreative, and nonviolent order of life called into question much of the values of early colonial New England and settler America by pointing to a different way of ordering relationships.

The story twists and turns from there. In the late eighteenth century, the Congregational Church itself undergoes a divisive split across lines drawn by the Holy Spirit. Some churches join the Great Awakening through the revivalist flames fanned by minister and soon-to-be renowned theologian Jonathan Edwards. Some, like the Shakers, anticipate Christ's imminent return. Some, also like the Shakers, are experiencing ecstatic states such as speaking in tongues, visions, and dancing. They are tasting a new feeling of freedom in Christ. These

Congregationalists coalesce with a larger movement called the
New Lights, often leaving the churches to join with Baptists and
other freewheelers. Together, such "New Lights" are pursuing
the Holy Spirit's revival amongst them and preparing to meet
Christ at his return, which seems just around the bend.

In 1780, a group of Protestants experience a mass conversion to the Shakers. Two nearby ministers visit the Shakers,
one a New Light Baptist preacher, the other a New Light
Presbyterian minister. These preachers tell their followers,
made up of numerous former Congregationalists, and about
370 convert to Shakerism. Such Christians already believed that
Christ was about to return, and meeting the Shakers confirmed
it for them because the Shakers testified in their experience
that Christ *had* already returned. As the Presbyterian minister
Samuel Johnson put it, "I first attended a meeting in Hancock,
praying to God that I might know the truth…[and] the substance of those gifts tended to show that the second appearing
of Christ was at hand."[129]

The Shakers believed with all their might that Christ had
come again, which led them to live and proclaim that the fullness
of life was here and that a depth dimension of love was available already. They taught us a passion for collective worship,
and they showed us that we didn't need to wait until the next
life to begin living values of nonviolence, simplicity, and community. Whether we call it Christ's Second Appearance, a new
birth, or utopia, they discovered humanity's spiritual birthright
of experiencing Christ now. And that's worth shaking about.

.   .   .

PREPARE FOR DEATH

As I pull up to the driveway for my pre-arranged hospice visit, the patients understand clearly why I am there. Some don't wish to speak with me, and that's okay; some wish to speak to me all day, which I politely decline. Whether they are a successful businessperson or a plumber in poverty, living in a mansion or a trailer, I visit them for one purpose—to provide spiritual support for their transition to death. I'm the hospice chaplain.

I don't have any magic rituals or gimmicky tricks to give, only a compassionate presence and willingness to listen. I don't view it as my job to foist Christianity on them if they don't already believe. I highlight instead the values and traditions that they state as important to them. Often, the patient just wants to talk and reminisce. Then there are the inevitable days when a patient is in too much pain to talk, and the only supportive gestures I can offer are a recitation of Psalm 23 and a friendly hand to hold.

The tenderness of someone's last weeks, days, and hours can be palpable. Sometimes it's anything but tender and the patient "rages against the dying of the light" (Dylan Thomas), but in my experience when a patient goes onto hospice, soon enough, the dying becomes both a shock, and—for those who dare embark upon it—a path of surrender.

Mary's anointing of Jesus's feet with oil in John's gospel seems to me like a hospice visit. It is slightly embarrassing in its raw vulnerability. There's the oil, the hair, the feet, and the emotional sensuality of the scene. It's almost as if she's saying her last goodbye.

In this story, Jesus is eating dinner in Bethany, close to Jerusalem, at the house of his dear friends Mary, Martha, and Lazarus. Lazarus—who has just traversed his own dying process in the preceding chapter, now is reclining at table and having a glass of wine. But even though Lazarus is with them again, Martha, Mary and their Jewish community are still grieving Lazarus's loss. You don't bounce back from a death that easily, even if the dead are resuscitated. They are angry at Jesus' failure to visit one last time which, the sisters insist, could have changed everything. Both sisters tell Jesus, "If you had been here, my brother would not have died" (John 11:32)—as if to say, "Jesus, where were you?"

Jesus' raising of Lazarus caused a commotion. How could it not? There was no YouTube live, no aggressive paparazzi to show up on the scene, but somehow, like gossip in a small town, word gets around. After this dramatic reversal of death, many people trusted what they witnessed and followed Jesus.

Many did not welcome the new possibilities emerging through Jesus' presence and mission. The political, religious elites known as the "temple leaders" called an emergency meeting because the movement seemed too hot to handle. "What are we accomplishing?" they said. "If we let the movement survive, it will only grow, and the Romans will come and take away our temple and nation" (John 11:47-8). The Jesus movement inevitably called into question the authority and primacy of Rome's power, and from their vantage point it was dangerous. The temple leaders built their careers and lives around the empire's domination. The high priest himself says what everyone else is thinking: "It's better for one person to die than for all of us" (John 11:47-53).

The myth of redemptive violence believes that violence solves problems, and here the religious and political professionals employ it to their brutal advantage. The logic is simple: Jesus is a threat and must be disposed of. His death will save us. Violence is the answer.

At risk to his life, Jesus returns to Bethany undercover. He knows where the political plot is headed. This is the beginning of the end. Or, if you affirm the unity of death and resurrection, as the gospels do, it's the beginning of the end which is a new beginning.

John's tale about the death of Jesus starts here. One life, Lazarus's life, is given a little more time. Another life, Jesus' life, is nearing the end of his time. Both call for acceptance.

Mary wiping Jesus' feet with oil and hair is beautiful and, for the onlookers, a bit embarrassing. It's like when someone wails with sustained grief at a funeral, and the rest of the people gathered don't know to respond. The person's guttural anguish is vulnerable, raw, and overpowering, and typical social and religious conventions do not prepare people for how to handle authentic heartbreak in ourselves or others. Often lament becomes a healing process for the grieving person to tune into the frequency of love, devotion, and grief, all in one.

Mary's anointing of Jesus is raw and vulnerable. It's also unashamedly erotic. Oil is pouring over the floor, running over Jesus' toes, trickling down Mary's neck. She caresses Jesus' feet with her hair. The scent fills the house.

What is this about? The disciples cannot at first make sense of it, and readers may not, either. We sympathize with Judas's fair point: "Why wasn't this perfume sold and the money given to the poor?" (John 12:5) He's saying, "We did not budget for this extravagant expense."

Anointing with oil is typically a ritual for a king, but Mary's anointing is anything but typical. In the Hebrew Bible, leaders are anointed as a way of declaring them to be the divinely-chosen ruler, such as when the prophet Samuel poured oil over a young, soon-to-be king David's head (1 Samuel 16:1-13). Would be-rulers also typically receive anointing on their heads, not their feet. Mary is up to something different, but the royal associations still ring in the background. Jesus, the story echoes, is the new king. Jesus, the story intones, is the Christ, which means the "anointed one." Jesus the anointed one, the early Christian story heralds, will also anoint by revealing all reality as holy.

"Leave her alone," Jesus says (John 12:7). You can hear the disciples' unnerved whispering. They know that Mary, like many hosts at whose tables they've sat, washed guests' feet countless times after dusty travels, and that *this* foot washing with oil pushes boundaries.

But it's Mary's devotion for Jesus that runs deep and true. After all, once Lazarus dies, Martha goes out to confront Jesus when he is on his way to their house—"Lord, if you had been here, my brother Lazarus would not have died" (John 11:21). Jesus' healing presence could have saved his friend and her brother. When it's Mary's turn to greet Jesus, she says the exact statement that Martha said, except she falls at his feet weeping while saying it. It's Mary's plea that moves Jesus to be stirred by his own grief and to ask where Lazarus's tomb is located. Mary's tears lead to those powerful two words that are also the most vulnerable in scripture: "Jesus wept" (John 11:35). It's Mary's intervention that convinces Jesus to raise Lazarus.

Mary is a disciple, a seeker of love in the way of Jesus. Before the joyful exuberance at seeing her brother Lazarus again can set in, she understands the events unfolding around Jesus. She knows he's going to die, she's accepted his fate, and so she pours oil on his feet, unabashedly imploring Jesus through her actions to—as the Song of Solomon puts it, "Set me as a seal over your heart, for love is as strong as death" (Song of Solomon 8:6). It's vulnerable and heartbreaking, a hospice ritual fit only for the most trusting intimacy.

Perhaps the intimacy of the scene is what unsettles Judas and the others. Judas' words are cloaked in social justice justification, a red herring to shield him from wholehearted devotion—"we could have used that money for the poor. Think about how many hungry people we could have fed!" (John 12:4).

The way Matthew's gospel tells it, Jesus challenges Judas right back: "The poor you will always have with you" (26:11), a verse often used by capitalists as a numbed acceptance of poverty's reality and inequality's injustice. But Jesus is anything but numb to the suffering around him. Instead, he's simply making a literal statement that "The poor will always be a part of this poor people's campaign." He's signaling that that his passionate life is almost at its end, but that the movement of heaven on earth in his name is inherently made up of the poor, the excluded, the sick, the demonized, and anyone else who wishes to unburden their heart.

We all traverse the archetypal path of death and resurrection. Jesus dies, and so do we. It's the one thing all humans have in common—that there is an end. Mary leads us in preparing for Christ's death and our own. Death in the world undoes us, and we stream tears. We look for purposeful action, and sometimes the wounds hurt so much that we even hide, like Judas, behind our otherwise commendable activities. Because if I were capable of feeling the grief trapped in my own body, how would I keep going? Yet somehow the grief opens a portal to the possible if we follow it all the way through.

There is no new life without the heartbreak and the letting go. There is no resurrection without first dying to all that separates us from love. Mary is anointing us, if we would not be too proud to let her hair smear oil on our wrinkled and worn feet. She knows full well what violence our world is capable of. She knows that each of us carries scars and loss. In spite of the pain, she anoints us for love, because only love gives us the courage to live and die in the way that God calls us to do.

·   ·   ·

LIVE FROM THE TRUE SELF

I have plenty of experience being both true and false. My false-
hood does not simmer from a stew of willful deceit, and I'd like
to think I'm a trustworthy person on which people can depend.
If I ever obfuscate or otherwise dance around truth, it's due to
an accidental misunderstanding or absentmindedness. I *meant* to
take those library books back, I swear. But my truthfulness does
not make me true.

Palm Sunday, the church service in which the Sunday
gathered wave palm branches and celebrate Christ's entrance
to Jerusalem, right before he dies, always feels both true and
false to me. The palm branches are an effective prop for kid-in-
volvement, and surely Jesus and the realm of divine peace and
justice are worth enthusiastic shouts of "Hosanna." That said,
I'm struck by the incongruity between the crowd's Hosanna
shouting and the upcoming "Good" Friday's bloody execution
and abandonment. The scripture headings call this passage a
"triumphal entry" of Jesus into the holy city, but Palm Sunday
in the larger story comes across like a misbegotten failure. My
palm branch waves at half-mast.

I suppose it feels false because I identify with the fickle
crowds. Jesus never pretends to be anyone other than who he
is, but the crowds and the disciples vacillate dramatically. These
same crowds who spread cloaks and branches on the ground,
who are singing Psalms with all their might (Mark 11:8-9), are
the same crowds who several days later will shout, "Crucify
him!" (15:13). It's easy to judge their volatile about-face from
a two-thousand-years-later perch, but I've at least done enough
self-inquiry to realize that I'm no different. The people's shouts
are my shouts, too.

Perhaps I can uncover my true and false self by way of my
generalized anxiety. I've been anxious for years, ever since tween

days. I'm not proud to admit it, but for a couple of decades, I obsessed with what people thought of me. I walked around with the constant terror of imminent rejection, rehearsing my internal assessments: Did she like me? Did he want to hang out with me? Was I—that ever torturous junior high and high school standard—*cool*? Even more, I sought *praise*. I led my Christian boarding school classmates in singing the praise song "Our God is an Awesome God" in chapel services, but I also wanted my peers to think *I* was awesome. In high school, I played guitar in various bands and—after I covered, say, "Better Man" by Pearl Jam at a community open mic, I yearned for adulation. Wasn't I amazing?!

The problem with building a self around other people's approval is that it always needs more approval. My quest for praise masked my psyche's gaping wounds that no friendship, peer group, or romance could ever hope to satisfy. What's more is that if I build my identity around what other people think of me, then my identity becomes *that* instead of who I really am.

In tenth grade, I gloried in all things Seattle grunge and loathed '80s glam rock—but when spending time with one friend who adored '80s rock, I fervently pledged my favorite band to be Def Leppard. It's a silly example, but I seared with myself with self-betrayal every time. Whoever I was was *not* that. Of course, now I can proudly sing all the words to "Pour Some Sugar on Me."

One way to contrast the true and false selves on Palm Sunday is to consider the nature of Jerusalem processions. After all, Jesus' procession on Palm Sunday is not the only procession to take place in Jerusalem on that fateful week of Jesus' death and resurrection. In *The Last Week*, biblical scholars John Dominic Crossan and Marcus Borg envision another possible procession underway at Jerusalem's west gate while pilgrims flock to the city for the Passover festival.[130] They point out that

Pilate would not have strolled into the city unannounced; he, too, would have entered via procession. And a Roman imperial procession would have been a sight to see: gold would have bedecked his horse, drumbeats would have pierced the air, soldiers would have been streaming in step as far as the eye could see. They'd be carrying their spears, some would be riding chariots, and the crowd would be shouting praises. Pilate's procession is intoxicating in its pomp and circumstance, which is to say that it is all false self. It magnifies its might, beats the war drum, and cannot imagine that anything other than the Empire could be more powerful.

Jesus' procession into Jerusalem echoes another procession from Jewish history. In the second century BCE, guerilla leader Judas Maccabeus and followers secured victory over their Seleucid imperial oppressors by taking the city and region. When they reclaimed the city, they *processed* into it. They marched to the Temple, rededicated and "cleansed" it from imperial occupation, all while carrying branches and palms. Their wielding of branches and palms is not a cute religious custom. It's a Ché Guavera-style victory lap.

For those of us who read the gospel centuries, empires and cultures later, Jesus' "triumphal entry" can be confusing. We miss the renegade street theater fun that gospel writer Mark is having. By having the crowd spread palms and branches on the ground, and placing Jesus riding upon a colt, Mark is offering a wink-nod to the revolutionary history of his Jewish tradition, mocking the imperial pomp of Roman processions, all while offering a loving and subversive third way. There are allusions to revolutionaries, verses that function as a wink and a nod to those who would have picked up on these signals.

Here are a couple of examples of Mark's allusions that the original hearers would have immediately understood. First, Jesus pauses near the Mount of Olives (Mark 11:1). A cranky

Jewish prophet named Zechariah had a vision about what would happen on the Mount of Olives that Jesus followers would not have forgotten. It went like this: "I will encamp at my temple to guard against marauding forces" (Zechariah 9:8), and "The Lord will fight against those nations, as he fights on a day of battle" (Zechariah 14:3), and on that day "His feet will stand on the Mount of Olives" (Zechariah 14:4). God will launch an offensive against Israel's imperial overlords, conquering and dividing plunder (14:1), and the liberation and freedom all begins at the Mount of Olives. Oh, and cantankerous Zechariah says, your king will be riding before you on a donkey (9:9).

Jesus' procession is different from both Roman and Jewish revolutionary parades. Gospel writer Mark alludes to both processions and overturns them. He's doing something different. Unlike Pilate, Jesus rides into Jerusalem vulnerable and undefended, from a peasant village called Nazareth. Instead of soldiers, he is marching alongside the poor, the formerly blind, the once-demon possessed, and women. He will even go to the temple, like Judas Maccabeus, and "cleanse it," but his direct action will not involve shedding blood other than his own (Mark 11:15-9). Jesus is certainly not Pilate, and Jesus also is not the violent revolutionary pursuing justice by any means necessary.

We can't blame palm wavers for getting caught up in the moment. We can offer sympathy to the crowds, too, knowing that each of us is prone to seek salvation by a quick fix. If only enlightenment were granted by a one and done prayer! Transformation is sadly slow. The fickle crowds may also stir sympathy for the many people in our day tempted towards nationalism, who drape themselves in swag and shout because they think a "strong man" will save them. Jesus is strong, but he's not the strong man who will kick ass the way the crowds think he will.

These days, my anxiety is still here, but I don't take it so seriously. I wake up and my critical mind is already buzzing with the things I should be doing, my to-dos and worries. But with a contemplative prayer sit and some exercise, the buzzing subsides and I enjoy that elusive sense of "me." Finally. It took me many years to realize that whoever "I" am, I haven't gone anywhere, I've been there the whole time! But contemplative prayer does something much more for me, too: it shows me that whoever "I" am, "I" am far more accepted and stretch far deeper than I could have dreamed.

The Trappist monk Thomas Merton used the phrases "true self and "false self" to describe two realities within us. The false self, he wrote in his classic *New Seeds of Contemplation* is:

> The self that exists only in my own egocentric desires…. Thus I use up my life in the desire for pleasure and the thirst for experiences, for power, honor, knowledge, and love, to clothe this false self and construct its nothingness into something objectively real. And I wind experiences around myself and cover myself with pleasures and glory like bandages in order to make myself perceptible to myself and to the world, as if I were an invisible body that could only become visible when something visible covered its surface.[131]

This false self is my insecure self, the self that will do anything to bask in the fading glow of praise and acceptance. And it's totally egocentric. Not because I'm a bad person, but because it's all about *me*. The true self is found within but guides me in the opposite direction. Instead of curving in upon myself, ever more obsessed with me, the true self opens me up to *You*, by which I mean God and the whole world.

The true self is infinitely expansive because it begins where I end—and that's where it finds God. Merton also wrote, "We become contemplatives when God discovers himself in us."[132] Salvation, before it became cheapened by mass production in the form of born again Christianity, tells us about identity. This lofty word "salvation" is a not a special prayer formula to wiggle into God's good graces, a morality game of doing or not-doing certain things, nor is it a worthiness contest about who can please a difficult God. Salvation is about knowing who we are.

But knowing who we are is far more than discovering the tastes and preferences of this individual "me." My likes and dislikes are rather particular, but they're not interesting. I'm discovering who I am in relationship with divine presence. As Merton puts it, "The secret of my identity is hidden in the love and mercy of God."[133] The divine presence is showing itself to me through me, but I rarely attune to it. Still, I am on my way.

.   .   .

PRAY AND LISTEN ON YOUR WAY

Why is contemplative prayer so needed in troubled times? Does the mystic generate any good in a world of climate crisis, racial trauma, nationalism, and violence? Unless contemplative prayer has something positive to offer to a suffering world, then it's all a ruse. Yet I hope I've convinced you that contemplative prayer, rather than avoiding the world's crises, instead grapples with them at their source—which is in our own consciousness.

Richard Rohr diagnoses both problem and solution in his book, *Immortal Diamond.* He writes about four splits from reality that contemplative prayer helps us overcome. I've found these to be very helpful and so I offer a brief commentary on each of his insights.

Rohr's first split is that "we split from our shadow self and pretend to be our idealized self."[134] We all present the self we desire to be to the world while airbrushing or repressing the unsavory aspects of the self. This is called, from Jungian psychology, the shadow self. Social media channels serve as online platforms to curate our image—the shadow self is anything we wouldn't dare post. Clergy or religious professionals like me pretend to be our idealized selves, too, perhaps more than most. We speak spiritual language and pray lofty prayers while our lives often tell a different truth. Even if we don't admit it to ourselves, we are guilty of thinking that a pulpit and a robe makes us separate from others, somehow more important.

The United States splits from their shadow self, too, as do most countries. What else is American exceptionalism than a split from the shadow self, and a failure to acknowledge the truth of Native American genocide, African slavery, and imperial wars? I once saw a graffiti sign on road trip that aptly said, "kill one person and it is murder, kill thousands and it is foreign policy." Contemplative prayer gives us the tools to see ourselves and reality as it is.

Split number two: "We split our minds from our body and soul and live in our minds."[135] Especially if we've spent time in academic contexts, it is very tempting to think that our minds represent the most vital aspect of us. In a time in which conspiracy theories swirl and basic facts seem to be up for grabs by various news media, it's important to name the brain's power and gifts. At the same time, much of Western philosophy's trajectory liberated reason to be independent and critical, all while neglecting bodies, and particularly marginalized bodies. The separation of bodies, souls, and minds, especially in Western Christianity created a tragic impasse: a confusion about the positive good, as well as the needed boundaries, of sexuality; an inability to listen to the wisdom that our bodies seek to speak; and an arrogant rejection of people whose minds do not work. As critical as ideas and arguments and books are, we will not take them with us when we die. Carrying for a person with Alzheimer's not only takes embodied spiritual discipline of the highest order, but it is also countercultural.

Split number three: "We split life from death and try to live our life without any death."[136] Much of us live our lives fueled by the fear of death. We attempt to accrue as much "stuff" as possible, whether in the form of experiences or material gain. This is perfectly understandable, but the pursuit of pleasure and comfort under the banner of life risks denying the ever-present simultaneous reality of death. Several years ago, I had the pleasure of spending time with someone who truly seemed free from death. His life-long spiritual practice had so cultivated self-surrender to love that, near the end of his life, he omitted a radiant presence that stirred a felt sense of love with many people who spent time with him. He showed me it is possible to embrace death as part of one's embrace of life. And in a way, contemplative prayer is nothing more than practicing the ego's death before the body's death. It's an opportunity to die before we die because we all die.

Split number four: "We split ourselves from other selves and try to live apart, superior, and separate."[137] A self-reliant culture rewards the self-reliant but at the cost of love. Individuals, groups, and nations are often tempted to stand off at a distance out of a false sense of superiority or fear. In high school, I refrained from hanging out with people, silently judging them while yearning to belong. Even though do-it-yourself Americans like to think otherwise, we are not separate. This truth applies to high-school social dynamics and global politics alike, for what is nationalism, other than a story of separateness? Nationalism tells a story of national uniqueness, often to the exclusion of other nations, or vulnerable peoples within nations, while wars evidence the brutal breakdown of shared human union.

Our world needs contemplative prayer to re-member us to the whole and holy ordinary. We discover our true selves in the Truest Self of God. And the Truest Self of God is dynamic, not separated from the relatedness of reality. Our lives and deaths, bodies and earth are united. The divine stream of love is always flowing in our direction, and every day is another chance to sip, savor it, and do our part to go along.

.   .   .

acknowledgments and permissions

Many of these chapters originated first as sermons. Special thanks to my friends at First Congregational Church, Williamstown, for providing an enlivening ministry context to explore the Bible together. You helped me find my voice. Thanks to Adam Bucko, who "saw" this project before I did and provided invaluable encouragement. Thanks to Jon Sweeney at Monkfish for his editing prowess and for believing in this project. Thanks to my fellow community members through the Center for Spiritual Imagination. With your friendship, I am beginning to live the contemplative life for which I've longed. Thanks to my wife Faith, who is the best soul friend and life partner I could imagine. "Find God at the Margins," was published in an earlier form in the Center for Action and Contemplation's *Oneing: Transformation,* Vol. 5, No. 1, Spring 2017. "Be Happy with Enough" was first published as "The Problem with More" in *Kosmos Journal,* September, 18, 2018. Several paragraphs from "Connect to the Source of Love" also appear in my chapter, "Contemplation and the Bible: Where, When, How?" in *Contemplation and Community: A Gathering of Fresh Voices for a Living Tradition* (New York: Crossroad Publishing, 2019).

endnotes

1   Thanks to Carl McColman's *The New Big Book of Christian Mysticism* for this quote (Minneapolis: Broadleaf Books, 2023), 27. The original can be found in Augustine, *Confessions*, Book XI, section 14, trans. Rex Warner (New York: Signet, 2001), 263.

2   Jean Gerson, as quoted by William Harmless, *Mystics* (New York: Oxford University Press, 2008), 5.

3   William James, as quoted in William Harmless, *Mystics*, 12.

4   Howard Thurman, *Mysticism and the Experience of Love* (Wallingford, PA: Pendle Hill, 1979), 6.

5   Brian McLaren, The Secret Message of Jesus: Uncovering the Truth that Could Change Everything (Nashville: Thomas Nelson, 2007), 37.

6   Richard Rohr, *Falling Upward: A Spirituality for the Two Halves of Life* (San Francisco: Jossey Bass, 2011), 13.

7   Tim Kreider, "It's Time to Stop Living the American Scam," July 7, 2022, *The New York Times*, accessed January 3, 2022.

8   Bernard of Clairvaux, as quoted in Susan Rakoczy, *Great Mystics and Social Justice: Walking on the Two Feet of Love* (New York: Paulist Press, 2006), 77–78.

9   Anonymous author, *The Cloud of Unknowing*, as quoted in Rakoczy, *Great Mystics and Social Justice: Walking on the Two Feet of Love*, 78.

10 John Calvin, *A Harmony of the Gospels Matthew, Mark and Luke, in John Calvin's New Testament Commentaries, Vol. 2*, eds. David W. Torrance and Thomas F. Torrance, trans. T.H.L. Parker (Grand Rapids: Eerdmans, 1989), 89.

11 Cynthia Bourgeault, *The Meaning of Mary Magdalene: Discovering the Woman at the Heart of Christianity* (Boulder, CO: Shambala Publications, 2010), 55.

12   Parker Palmer, *The Active Life: A Spirituality of Work, Creativity, and Caring* (San Francisco: Jossey Bass, 1990), 15.

13   Thomas Merton, as quoted in Michael Mott, *The Seven Mountains of Thomas Merton* (Boston: Houghton Mifflin, 1984), 172.

14   Mott, *The Seven Mountains of Thomas Merton*, 172.

15   Thomas Merton, *The Sign of Jonas* (San Diego: Harcourt Brace, 1981), 162.

16   Thomas Merton, "Is the World a Problem?" *Contemplation in a World of Action* (New York: Image, 1971), 159.

17   Kathleen Tarr, "From the Inner Frontier to the Last Frontier: Thomas Merton's 1968 Alaska Journey," *The Merton Seasonal: A Quarterly Review*, Vol. 44, No. 4, Winter 2019.

18   Thomas Merton, *Conjectures of a Guilty Bystander* (Garden City, NY: Image, 1968), 157.

19   Thomas Merton, "Letter to Pope John XXIII, November 10, 1958, *The Hidden Ground of Love: The Letters of Thomas Merton on Religious Experience and Social Concerns* (New York: Harcourt Brace Jovanovich, 1993), 482.

20   Brian McLaren, *The Secret Message of Jesus: Uncovering the Truth that Could Change Everything* (Nashville: Thomas Nelson, 2007), 37; also see John Ashton, *Understanding the Fourth Gospel* (New York: Oxford University Press, 2007), 400-2.

21   Barbara Brown Taylor, *An Altar in the World: A Geography of Faith* (New York: HarperOne, 2009), 15.

22   Diana Butler Bass, *Christianity After Religion: The End of Church and the Birth of a New Spiritual Awakening* (New York: HarperOne, 2012), 98.

23   See "Dionysius: Celestial Hierarchy 2," in Bernard McGinn, ed., *The Essential Writings of Christian Mysticism* (New York: Random House, 2006), 151.

24   Parker Palmer, *The Active Life: A Spirituality of Work, Creativity, and Caring* (San Francisco: Jossey Bass, 1990), 17.

25   Beverly Lanzetta, *The Monk Within: Embracing a Sacred Way of Life* (Sebastopol, CA: Blue Sapphire Books, 2018), 13.

26 Barbara Holmes, *Joy Unspeakable: Contemplative Practices of the Black Church* (Minneapolis: Fortress Press, 2004), 69.

27 Richard Rohr, *The Universal Christ: How a Forgotten Reality Can Change Everything We See, Hope For, and Believe* (New York: Convergent, 2021), 33.

28 Merton, *Contemplation in a World of Action*, 152.

29 Howard Thurman, *Footprints of a Dream: The Story of the Church for the Fellowship of All Peoples* (Eugene, OR: Wipf & Stock, 2009), 77.

30 Quoted in Albert J. Raboteau, *American Prophets: Seven Religious Radicals and Their Struggle for Social and Political Justice* (Princeton: Princeton University Press, 2016), 109.

31 Howard Thurman, *With Head and Heart: The Autobiography of Howard Thurman* (San Diego: Harcourt Brace, 1979), 160.

32 Thurman, *With Head and Heart*, 159.

33 Novalis, as quoted in Dorothy Sölle, *The Silent Cry: Mysticism and Resistance* (Minneapolis: Fortress Press, 2001), 9.

34 André Vauchez, *Francis of Assisi: The Life and Afterlife of a Medieval Saint* (New Haven: Yale University Press, 2012), 271-75.

35 *Little Flowers of St. Francis*, trans. Raphael Brown (New York: Doubleday, 1991), 89.

36 Thomas Berry, *The Great Work: Our Way Into the Future* (New York: Bell Tower, 199), 159.

37 Ann Larkin Hansen, *The Organic Farming Manual: A Comprehensive Guide to Starting and Running a Certified Organic Farm* (North Adams, MA: Storey Publishing, 2010), 24.

38 William Harmless, "Mystic as Multimedia Artist: Hildegard of Bingen," *Mystics* (New York: Oxford University Press, 2008), 59-78.

39 As quoted in William Harmless, *Mystics* (New York: Oxford University Press, 2008), 73-4. See also the helpful description of "viriditas" in *Hildegard of Bingen, The Letters of Hildegard of Bingen: Volume 1*, trans. Joseph Baird (New York: Oxford University Press, 1998), 7.

40 Richard Rohr, *Immortal Diamond: The Search for Our True Self* (San Francisco: Jossey-Bass, 2013), 84.

41   Hildegard of Bingen, *Scivias* (New York: Paulist Press, 1990), 525.

42   Peter V. Loewen, "From the Roots to the Branches: Greenness in the Preaching of Hildegard of Bingen and the Patriarchs," in Jennifer Bain, ed., *The Cambridge Companion to Hildegard of Bingen*, (New York: Cambridge University Press, 2021), 130.

43   Marcus Chown, *What a Wonderful World: One Man's Attempt to Explain the Big Stuff* (London: Faber, 2013), Kindle Location 3591, xiii, 284, 292.

44   J. Philip Newell, *Sounds of the Eternal: A Celtic Psalter* (Grand Rapids: Eerdmans, 2002), 29.

45   Walter Wink, *Naming the Powers: The Language of Power in the New Testament* (Philadelphia: Fortress Press, 1984), 28.

46   Ilia Delio, *The Unbearable Wholeness of Being: God, Evolution, and the Power of Love* (Maryknoll, NY: Orbis Books, 2013), 12.

47   Karin Figala, "Newton's Alchemy," in *The Cambridge Companion to Newton*, eds. George E. Smith, Bernard Cohen, and Irwin Bernard Cohen (New York: Cambridge University Press, 2002), 370.

48   Ilia Delio, *Simply Bonaventure: An Introduction to His Life, Thought, and Writing* (Hyde Park, NY: New City Press, 2001, 2013), chapter 2.

49   Denis Edwards, *The God of Evolution: A Trinitarian Theology* (Mahwah, NJ: Paulist Press, 1999), 21, 23.

50   Rik Van Nieuwenhove, *Jan Van Ruusbroec: Mystical Theologian of the Trinity* (Notre Dame, IN: Notre Dame University Press, 2003), 82-3.

51   Bill Leonard, *The Homebrewed Guide to Church History* (Minneapolis: Fortress Press, 2017), 68.

52   Justo Gonzalez, *A History of Christian Thought* (Nashville: Abingdon Press, 1970), 281-82.

53   John Muir, *Nature Writings* (New York: Library of America, 1997), 34.

54   Muir, *Nature Writings*, 238.

55   John Muir, *My First Summer in the Sierra* (Boston: Houghton Mifflin, 1911), 169.

56   Muir, *Nature Writings*, 212.

57   Eduard Lohse, *Colossians and Philemon*, trans. William R. Pehlmann and Robert J. Karris (Philadelphia: Fortress Press, 1971), 51-2.

58 Richard Rohr, *The Universal Christ: How a Forgotten Reality Can Change Everything We See, Hope For, and Believe* (New York: Convergent, 2021), 15.

59 Rohr, *The Universal Christ*, chapter 1.

60 Lohse, *Colossians and Philemon*, 53.

61 James McAuley, "The fall of Notre Dame is a body blow to Paris and all it represents," *Washington Post*, April 15, 2019. Accessed February 6, 2023.

62 Mykal Vincent and Carmen Poe, "Fundraiser for black churches destroyed by arson surpasses $2 million," Action News 5, April 18, 2019. Accessed January 7, 2023.

63 Wendell Berry, "Manifesto: The Mad Farmer Liberation Front," *Collected Poems, 1957–1982* (San Francisco: North Point Press, 1985), 151-52.

64 John Dominic Crossan and Sarah Sexton Crossan, *Resurrecting Easter: How the West Lost and the East Kept the Original Easter Vision* (New York: HarperCollins, 2018), 64-5, 84-5.

65 Crossan and Crossan, *Resurrecting Easter*, 110-11.

66 Quoted in Elizabeth Johnson, *Ask the Beasts: Darwin and the God of Love* (New York: Bloomsbury, 2014), 209.

67 Wendell Berry, "Manifesto: The Mad Farmer Liberation Front," *Collected Poems, 1957–1982* (San Francisco: North Point Press, 1985), 152.

68 James Baldwin, *Another Country* (New York: Vintage International, 1960), 340.

69 See David Leeming, *James Baldwin: A Biography* (New York: Arcade Publishing, 1994), chapter 21 "Africa and The Fire Next Time."

70 James Baldwin, "My Dungeon Shook," in *Collected Essays* (New York: Library of America, 1998), 292.

71 Baldwin, "My Dungeon Shook, *Collected Essays*, 293.

72 Baldwin, "The Fire Next Time, in *The Price of the Ticket: Collected Nonfiction: 1948–1985* (New York: St. Martin's Prress, 1985), 375.

73 Martin Luther King Jr., "Beyond Vietnam," in *A Call to Conscience: The Landmark Speeches of Dr. Martin Luther King, Jr.*, eds. Clayborne Carson and Kris Shepard (New York: Warner Books, 2001), 160-61.

74 Baldwin, "My Dungeon Shook," *Collected Essays*, 294.

75 Eddie Glaude, *Begin Again: James Baldwin's America and Its Urgent Lessons for Our Own* (New York: Crown, 2020), 110.

76 James Baldwin, No Name in the Street, in *Collected Essays* (New York: Library of America, 1998), 474.

77 Baldwin, "My Dungeon Shook," *Collected Essays*, 294.

78 *Evelyn Underhill: Essential Writings*, ed. Emilie Griffin (Maryknoll, NY: Orbis Books, 2003), 26.

79 Brian McLaren, "A New Kind of Unity," Emerging Christianity conference (Albuquerque: Center for Action and Contemplation), 2010.

80 Cynthia Bourgeault, *The Wisdom Jesus: Transforming Heart and Mind—a New Perspective on Christ and His Message* (Boston: Shambhala Publications, 2008), 33.

81 Sociological definitions of margins from Warren Carter, *Matthew and the Margins: A Sociopolitical and Religious Reading* (Maryknoll, NY: Orbis, 2000), 45.

82 Jeremy Thomson, "Humans did come out of Africa, says DNA," December 7, 2000, *Nature*. Accessed online January 7, 2023.

83 David Roediger, *How Race Survived U.S. History* (New York: Verso, 2008), x-xi.

84 Ta-Nehisi Coates, "The Case for Reparations," *The Atlantic*, June 2014.

85 Ched Myers, *Binding the Strong Man: A Political Reading of Mark's Story of Jesus* (Maryknoll, NY: Orbis Books, 1988), 271-74.

86 See Jordan Winthrop, *White Over Black: American Attitudes Toward the Negro, 1550-1812* (New York: Norton, 1977), 15–16

87 Clarice Martin, "The Haustafeln (Household Codes)" in Cain Felder Hope, ed., *Stony the Road We Trod: African American Biblical Interpretation* (Minneapolis: Fortress Press, 1991), 215.

88 James Weldon Johnson, "The Creation," *God's Trombones* (New York: Viking Press, 1927, 1955).

89 Catherine Keller, *Face of the Deep: A Theology of Becoming* (New York: Routledge, 2003).

90 Keller, *Face of the Deep*, 183

91 Neil deGrasse Tyson, *Astrophysics for People in a Hurry* (New York: Norton, 2017), 21.

92 Keller, *Face of the Deep*, xvii.

93 Keller, *Face of the Deep*, 183.

94 "Dark Matter," ESA/Hubble Word Bank, www.esahubble.org/wordbank/dark-matter. Accessed January 9, 2023.

95 Barbara Holmes, *Race and the Cosmos: An Invitation to View the World Differently* (Albuquerque: CAC Publishing, 2020), 147.

96 John of the Cross, "The Dark Night," *The Poems of John of the Cross* (Chicago: University of Chicago Press, 1979), 19.

97 As quoted by Denise Levertov, "Annunciation," *A Door in the Hive* (New York: New Directions, 1989), 86.

98 Rob Bell, "Rob Bell's Live at Largo Christmas Show," The Robcast, Episode 178, podcast audio, https://robbell.podbean.com/e/rob-bells-largo-christmas-show-with-the-band-joseph/.

99 Denise Levertov, "Annunciation," *A Door in the Hive*, 86.

100 Elizabeth Johnson, *Truly Our Sister: A Theology of Mary in the Communion of Saints* (New York: Continuum, 2003), 251.

101 Valerie Kaur, "Watch Night Speech: Breathe and Push," January 8, 2017, https://valariekaur.com/2017/01/watch-night-speech-breathe-push/. Accessed July 16, 2023.

102 Richard Rohr, *Great Themes of Paul: Life as Participation* (Cincinnati: Franciscan Media, 2002), Audible version.

103 Walter Wink, *Engaging the Powers* (Minneapolis: Fortress Press, 2017), 64.

104 Edwin Muir, "The Incarnate One," Malcolme Guite, *Word in the Wilderness: A Poem a Day for Lent and Easter* (London: Canterbury Press, 2014), 129.

105 Quoted in Warren Carter, *Matthew and the Margins: A Sociopolitical and Religious Reading* (Maryknoll, NY: Orbis Books, 2000), 74.

106 Ulrich Luz, *Matthew 1-7: A Commentary* (Minneapolis, MN: Fortress Press, 2007) 106-07.

107 Gregory Smith, "About Three-in-Ten U.S. Adults are Now Religiously Unaffiliated," December 14, 2021, Pew Research Center. Accessed February 6, 2023.

108 Elizabeth Bloch-Smith, "Solomon's Temple: The Politics of
     Ritual Space," in *Sacred Time, Sacred Place: Archaeology and the Religion
     of Israel*, ed. Barry M. Gittlen (Winona Lake, IN: Eisenbrauns,
     2002), 85.

109 Raimon Panikkar, *The Rhythm of Being: The Unbroken Trinity*
     (Maryknoll, NY: Orbis Books, 2010), 180.

110 Denis Edwards, *Jesus the Wisdom of God: An Ecological Theology*
     (Maryknoll, NY: Orbis Books, 1995), 39-41.

111 Richard Rohr, "Creation as the Body of God," in Llewellyn
     Vaughan-Lee, ed., *Spiritual Ecology: The Cry of the Earth* (Point
     Reyes, CA: The Golden Sufi Center, 2016), 258.

112 Matthew Fox, *The Coming of the Cosmic Christ* (San Francisco:
     Harper & Row, 1988), 1.

113 Rob Bell, *What We Talk About When We Talk About God* (New York:
     HarperOne, 2013), 148–49.

114 Quoted in Richard Lewis, ed., *The Way of Silence: The Prose and
     Poetry of Basho* (New York: Dial Press, 1970), 82.

115 Jean Gerson, quoted in William Harmless, *Mystics* (New York:
     Oxford University Press, 2005), 5.

116 Jean Gerson, quoted in *Brian Patrick McGuire, Jean Gerson and the
     Last Medieval Reformation* (University Park, PA: Pennsylvania State
     University Press, 2010), 94.

117 Jean Gerson, *Early Works*, trans. Brian Patrick McGuire (New
     York: Paulist Press, 1998), 80.

118 Adam Frank, *The Constant Fire: Beyond the Science vs. Religion Debate*
     (Berkeley: University of California Press, 2009), 152.

119 Gordon Kaufman, *In the Beginning . . Creativity* (Minneapolis:
     Fortress, 2004), 71.

120 John de Gruchy, *Christianity, Art and Transformation* (Cambridge,
     UK: Cambridge University Press, 2001), 25.

121 Karl Barth, as quoted in de Gruchy, *Christianity, Art and
     Transformation*, 122.

122 Ronald Rolheiser, *The Holy Longing: The Search for Christianity
     Spirituality* (New York: Image, 2014), 3.

123 John of the Cross, *The Ascent of Mount Carmel in John of the Cross: Selected Writings*, trans. Kieran Kavanaugh (Mahwah, NJ: Paulist Press, 1987), 64.

124 John of the Cross, *Selected Writings*, 152.

125 Sarah Coakley, *The New Asceticism: Sexuality, Gender, and the Quest for God* (London: Bloomsbury Publishing, 2015), 141.

126 James Finley and Richard Rohr, *Intimacy: The Divine Ambush* (Center for Action and Contemplation: 2013), audio teaching.

127 As quoted in Iain Matthew, *The Impact of God: Soundings from St. John of the Cross* (London: Hodder & Stoughton, 1995, 2010), 57-8.

128 Stephen J. Stein, *The Shaker Experience in America: A History of the United Society of Believers* (New Haven: Yale University Press, 1994); and Richard Francis, *Ann the Word: The Story of Ann Lee, Female Messiah, Mother of the Shakers, the Woman Clothed with the Sun* (New York: Arcade Publishing, 2001).

129 Samuel Johnson in *The Shakers: Two Centuries of Spiritual Reflection*, ed. Robley Edward Whitson (Mahwah, NJ: Paulist Press, 1983), 53.

130 Marcus J. Borg and John Dominic Crossan, *The Last Week: The Day-by-Day Account of Jesus's Final Week in Jerusalem* (San Francisco: HarperSanFrancisco, 2006), 3.

131 Thomas Merton, *New Seeds of Contemplation* (New York: New Directions, 1961), 34-5.

132 Merton, *New Seeds*, 39.

133 Merton, *New Seeds*, 35.

134 Richard Rohr, *Immortal Diamond: The Quest for the True Self* (San Francisco: Jossey-Bass, 2013), 29.

135 Rohr, *Immortal Diamond*, 29.

136 Rohr, *Immortal Diamond*, 29.

137 Rohr, *Immortal Diamond*, 29.

MARK LONGHURST is a writer and "ordinary mystic." He is a member of the new monastic Community of the Incarnation and works as the publications manager at the Center for Action and Contemplation. A former pastor, he served United Church of Christ churches for ten years and worked as a faith-based social justice activist in the Boston area for ten more. A graduate of Harvard Divinity School, and a longtime yoga-practitioner, he runs two Substack newsletters at marklonghurst.substack.com. Mark lives in western Massachusetts with his family.

Printed in the USA
CPSIA information can be obtained
at www.ICGtesting.com
JSHW021135271024
72352JS00042B/100

9 781958 972519